A Journey of Courage

A Journey of Courage

The Amazing Story of Sister Dorothy Stang

MICHELE MURDOCK

SISTERS OF NOTRE DAME DE NAMUR

OHIO PROVINCE

THE SISTER DOROTHY STANG FUND

A Journey of Courage is published by the
Sisters of Notre Dame de Namur
Ohio Province

The Sister Dorothy Stang Fund
Cincinnati, Ohio

Sister Dorothy Stang's biography is based on factual information
provided by the Sisters of Notre Dame de Namur and the Stang
Family. Certain events were fictionalized by the author to
compensate for lack of transitional information. The Sisters of
Notre Dame de Namur and Stang family have approved the book

A Journey of Courage
Copyright © Michele Murdock, 2009
All rights reserved
www.michelemurdock.com

Printed in the United States of America
13 12 11 10 09   5 4 3 2 1

ISBN 978-1-61539-780-8

This book was printed on acid-free paper and meets the
guidelines for permanence and durability of the
Council on Library Resources.

Typeset by Copperline Book Services in Arno Pro.
Printed by Thomson-Shore, Inc.
Printed in the United States of America
2009

To the memory of my cousin, Jackie Virgalla, who had an unwavering faith in God. Her generosity allowed me to take the time to do the necessary research and travel to Ohio and Brazil. I can still see her big brown eyes widen when I explained the project I was about to undertake: "Oh, *that* sounds great!"

Contents

Introduction

WHEN I WAS a small child, perhaps four years old, my parents and I visited a Montessori preschool north of New York City to see about my attending. Inside the beautiful stone building, casement windows opened onto views of the deep blue Hudson River. Sweet, smiling nuns helped little girls like me, who were busy coloring with crayons from buckets, cutting colorful paper with blunt-nosed scissors, and painting on large easels. This school would suit me perfectly, I thought.

One of the Sisters showed us the classroom that would be mine. She touched me on the shoulder and asked if I would like to go to school there. I wanted nothing more. In the end, I did not attend the school. I'm not sure why. But I still remember the place over sixty years later, I think, because the nuns were so very kind to me, and I felt safe there.

My guess is that the peasants of the northern area of Brazil where the nun Dorothy Stang worked felt safe in her care, too. From the moment I first read about Dorothy, a Sister of Notre Dame de Namur, I knew I had to find out more about her. I thrust myself into research, into a world of nuns who don't wear habits, who walk along forest trails in jungles looking for peasant farmers, helping them create community and defend their land. And these Sisters share Gospel stories, relating them to the peasants' daily struggles.

Some of these nuns also support and participate in peaceful demonstrations, advocating for better housing or tax relief for the poor. They support immigrants, sheltering them if necessary. Despite their long work hours, they laugh and sing as they carry out their mission to "be an option for the poor." Some of the nuns are tall and stately, others short and stooped. They deal with diabetes, arthritis, and osteoporosis. Few are younger than fifty-five. They have PhDs and have built chapels and schools in faraway places; they sit on community boards and start worldwide peace organizations. They are focused advocates for social justice.

Where are the young nuns? The ones I know personally are in Brazil, working with the poor and following the example of their older Sisters. They study hard. They work with seriously disadvantaged children, engaging them in art therapy. They work in clinics with sick adults and with those suffering with AIDS and alcoholism. They are serious students of the Bible, of the journey of Jesus Christ, of the kind of faith that has renewed mine. They know how to reach people in need. They are getting advanced degrees in social work and in early childhood education; one I know is studying to be a lawyer.

They are a small group, and you will not recognize them by their outfits or their solemn and silent faces, though they may be wearing crosses. You will know them because they smile and greet you warmly. They are in Africa and in Peru and Guatemala and Alaska and Brooklyn and Baltimore and Cincinnati. They live in the present; they have more work than they can do in any one day or even any one year. They are happy in community with each other and happy with their jobs. I pray that they can show the rest of us how to keep our heads on straight and our hearts determined.

SEVERAL SISTERS helped me with this book. At the top of the list are Sisters Elizabeth Bowyer and Joan Krimm, who gave me their approval to write and publish this book. We have become good friends, and I cherish the time I have spent with them and all that I have learned from them.

I also thank the archivist and historian Sister Louanna Orth, whose copy machine I almost ruined reproducing more than 100 of Dorothy's letters. Those letters allowed me to create the introductory incident in "A Farmer Remembers," and the dialogue throughout to make her story and life come alive. The book is based on Sister Dorothy's true experiences.

I met several times with Sister Rebeca Spires, a gifted linguist and Dorothy's good friend in Brazil. Like the others involved in the peasants' struggle — Jo Depwig, Jane Dwyer, and Katy Webster and several other sisters — Becky is inspiring, gracious, and a font of information. I thank them all for their help. I also must thank Sister Roseanne Murphy, SND de N. I am indebted to her for the early research she did looking into Dorothy's life and work in Brazil.

I cannot forget my "Brazilian daughters," whom I met in 2007. Lucyane, Rosinha, Josi, Maria Wagner and Wanessa were in various stages of formation — that is, of becoming Sisters of Notre Dame de Namur. And there are still others who are further along the path. All are full of a joyful determination to better the lives of the poor in a million different ways.

Determination is the banner of the Stang family. No one has stepped up to work on delivering justice to Dorothy's memory more than David Stang, one of her twin younger brothers. Supported by all the other family members, he has made numerous trips to Brazil and kept up the fight to expose the injustice of the rich ranchers and the impunity granted them in their illegal fight with the poor farmers.

Many of the Stangs specifically David, Marguerite Hohm and Barb Richardson gave me valuable information about their sister and extended their friendship to me as well. I am grateful to all of them. Then there are the writers who read my work and sped me on the way, encouraging me to follow my passion for this woman I never knew in person: Suzanne Chazin, Marthe Jocelyn, and Carol Henderson.

I want to thank my friends who encouraged me and gasped

each time I told the story — Dana, Sarah, Lynn, Sheri, Kathy and Hannah, who read the manuscript, and many others who cheered me along. I owe special gratitude to my college friend Maureen Egen, the esteemed past publisher of the Time Warner Book Group who guided me on this, my first publishing venture, and who is herself a devoted fan of this order of Sisters.

Finally, my husband, Peter, and my son, Mike, thought it quite terrific that after all these years of nurturing them and heading a communications firm in New York, I would turn to this project. It is because of Peter's unending patience and Mike's enthusiasm that I finished. I would not have done it without their support.

Dorothy and her friends have changed my life by showing me that tireless devotion to the poor and needy can exist alongside great happiness, that deep faith builds courage, and that living simply can offer the richest life ever.

Latin America and the
States of Brazil

Venezuela

Guyana

French
Guiana

Suriname

Columbia

Raoraima

Ecuador

Amapá

Pará

Amazon River

Brazil

Amazonas

Pará

Maranhão

Ceará

Rio Grande
do Norte

Peru

Acre

Piauí

Paraíba

Pernmabuco

Rondonia

Tocantin

Alagoas

Sergipe

Mato Grosso

Bahia

Goias

Bolivia

Brasilia

Minas Gerais

Mato Grosso
du Sul

Espirito Santo

Sáo Paulo

Rio de Janeiro

Chile

Paraguay

Paraná

Santa Catarina

Rio Grande
do Sul

Argentina

Uruguay

Latin America

States of Brazil

Where Dorothy Traveled

0   500 Kilometers

0   500 Miles

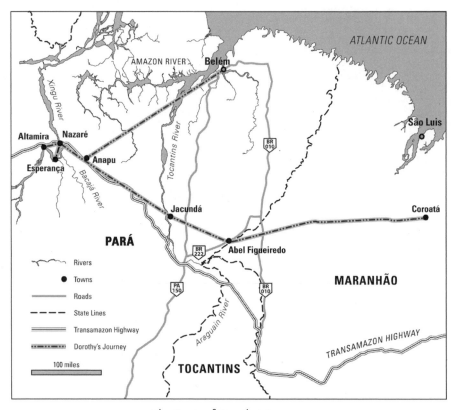

The Route of Dorothy's Journey.
Dorothy Stang began in Coroatá and travelled west. From Anapu
she went often to Belém, the capital of the state of Pará.

Foreword

The following is an excerpt from a letter written in 1989 by Sister Claire Callahan, head of missions for South America and Africa for the order of the Sisters of Notre Dame de Namur. Sister Claire wrote the letter during a trip to Brazil.

I OPENED a guidebook on my flight to Brazil: "The sea breeze is gentle, the sun is ever present . . . and the seafood is delicious." . . . It advised me to find regional roots and herbs to spice my food and perfume my closets and to taste a sort of salty tapioca pudding containing shrimp and hot peppers and the sauce served with it. . . . It showed sleek brilliantly colored images of stately hotels, graceful sailboats, ancient architecture, and the world's finest cuisine.

I couldn't find a word about . . . Nazaré. There was no mention made of the rape of the forests, nor the waterless areas where the local people scrounge out an existence, nor did it alert me to the dusty roads, the leaking buses, or the villages that have never had power for light or cooking or health care.

The Brazil I encountered was the Brazil where our Sisters live and minister and share life with a portion of the twenty million adults who are illiterate and the five million children to whom education is denied in the eighth-richest country in the world! Believe me, there was little resemblance to the tourist-tempting brochure; but there was another life, another country, another mentality that we, who have embraced the "option for the poor," live out in Brazil through the persons of our Sisters there.

A Farmer Remembers

SISTER DOROTHY STANG smiled down on Cicero from the photo on the wall of his home. He smoothed the front of his clean, white T-shirt. It bore another picture of Dorothy with her slogan, "The Death of the Forest is the end of our lives."

The farmer swallowed hard. His wife watched closely.

"*Querido*, you look good," she said, "and you know what you want to say. Go on now. Dorothy would have been pleased."

The date was February 12, 2006. Exactly one year before, Dorothy had been walking along the dirt road outside on her way to a meeting. She had called out to the farmer at his open door: "Cicero, I'm ready, are you?"

"My daughter is sick and I don't want to leave her," he told her. "My wife should be back any minute. I will follow you as soon as she returns."

"OK. I hope your daughter feels better. Just meet me as soon as you can."

A fine mist was falling as Dorothy walked on. She carried her cloth bag, which held her Bible and some papers. She moved briskly because of the rain. Cicero stepped out of his house a few minutes later. He walked fast, trying to catch up with her.

At a bend in the path, Dorothy saw two men step out of the forest; they had been spreading grass seed for cattle. She wondered what they were doing there so early in the morning. Nevertheless, she greeted them and then passed by.

One of the men called out: "Sister Dorothy!"

She turned around and saw that he had a gun. She pulled a Bible from her bag and held up the other hand as if to ward off a blow. She read aloud for a moment.

Cicero was catching up to Dorothy just as the first shot rang out. He jumped behind a tree and watched Dorothy fall to the ground face down. One of the men walked over to her and fired five more shots into her body.

"Oh my God," Cicero whispered. "They've shot Sister Dorothy."

He could see the gunmen, the *pistoleiros*, but they could not see him behind the tree. They were looking at the body lying in the red dirt. Cicero wanted to help Dorothy, yet he knew they would kill him too if he stepped out. His whole body felt like lead.

He turned around and began to run back down the road to seek help and to escape the men. Cicero needed to tell the other farmers what had happened; they were waiting for him in *Esperança* — at the settlement called "Hope."

He ran through the forest, taking trails that he knew. His breathing was heavy, and tears were choking him. He tripped over vines and gasped for air; still, he tried to run faster. He burst through the undergrowth into a clearing where farm families were waiting for him and Dorothy.

"She is dead," he sobbed. "She's dead. They shot her . . . they shot Sister Dorothy! Get the police. Dorothy . . . is dead."

Men, women, and children gathered around him, trying to comprehend what had happened. Some started screaming and crying: "Who did it? Where is she now? Let's go get her . . . let's get the killers!"

"No, you can't," Cicero said. "They will get you too. They have a gun. That's why I ran."

Another farmer, Reginaldo, jumped on his motorcycle to

drive to Anapu, Dorothy's hometown, to get the police. Everyone knew they were not to move a body until the police came. This farmer would notify the mayor and any others who could help. There were no phones at Esperança.

The peasants were all stunned by the news. They talked among themselves and wept.

Who would shoot a nun? How could anyone shoot this woman who had educated them and been their spiritual guide for almost twenty-five years?

Most of the peasant farmers knew that Dorothy's life had been threatened. They had feared that she would be killed for helping them learn to defend their human rights. Still, they were stunned, shocked that their friend had been ruthlessly murdered.

Now, a year later, Cicero walked to the site of Dorothy's memorial service. He sighed, remembering how afraid he had been that morning a year ago. Dorothy had come to the small community the night before to help the settlers deal with a vicious land dispute. The rancher, who claimed the land was his, was known for his illegal activities.

It had taken all day for the police to get to Esperança; they finally arrived toward evening. Cicero, who had officially reported the murder of Sister Dorothy Stang, led them to her body. She was still lying there in the muddy road, the body unmoved, skin softened by the gentle rain, her blood still seeping into the dirt.

Today, Cicero was prepared to speak about his family's love for Dorothy, how she had taught them to dream — and to make decisions. He missed her so much.

He cleared his throat, touched the mahogany tree planted above her grave on the bank of the Anapu River, and spoke to those gathered to commemorate the day.

"This tree represents our beloved *Dorothea*'s belief that the rain forest can be saved," he said. "With her smiling eyes and her soft voice, she taught us that we can learn to treat the land and its creatures with the same respect that we all deserve."

Cicero's voice cracked. He wiped a tear from his eye, tugged at his shirt, and bowed his head.

PART ONE

Before Brazil, 1931–1966

CHAPTER ONE

Who Was Dorothy Stang?

WHO WAS this extraordinary woman who helped poor peasants and slum dwellers become small farmers in northern Brazil? What was it about her that made a rich man so angry that he would pay to have her killed?

Dorothy Stang was born in 1931 in Shiloh, Ohio, a rural community just outside the city of Dayton. She was the fourth child born to Henry and Edna Stang. Eventually, Dot, as she was affectionately called, would have eight brothers and sisters. A large family like Dot's was not unusual in this part of Ohio, where many Catholic families lived. Everyone who knew the Stangs admired Henry and Edna's strong faith. The whole family trooped, two by two, into Mass every Sunday.

In addition to mothering nine children, Edna made time to care for sick neighbors and cousins and organize an annual charity event, the St. Rita's School fall festival. Henry had graduated from the University of Dayton and worked as a chemical engineer and a gardener.

Dot was known as the neighborhood "Pied Piper," attracting many friends to play in her backyard. She was a good athlete, and her sister Norma says she was the "leader" in the family. Others recall that she was "feisty" and even "ornery" at times. She definitely loved an escapade.

One summer day, when she was about ten years old, Dot was dutifully practicing the piano in a room at the back of the house. She heard bees buzzing outside; the scent of honeysuckle drifted in. She had promised her mother she would practice for half an

Dorothy , age 10 in 1941

The Stang Family in Ohio, Dorothy at right

hour — thirty *whole* minutes, she thought. She squirmed on the piano stool and sighed.

Overcome by the tedium of piano practice and the knowledge that her bike was just outside, Dot opened the window screen and climbed out. She jumped the few feet to the ground, grabbed the bike, and sped down the rolling hill that ran in front of her house.

"Whoopee, I'm free!" she shouted.

The breeze ruffled her hair, and the bike seemed to sail. *I'll go back soon,* she promised herself. *There'll be only fifteen minutes left when I return.*

And at that moment, she hit a bump and flew over the handlebars, landing face first. She sat up, moved her legs, then her hands and arms. Nothing seemed to be broken. She touched her chin and felt blood. When she tried to wipe the blood from her mouth, she found a dangling front tooth!

Oh boy, she thought. *This will be hard to explain.*

Not hearing piano music, Edna had gone outside to look for her daughter, just in time to see Dot walking the bike back up the drive. Her head was hanging down and she was holding something in her hand. Her mother looked at the scrapes and the bloody chin. She quickly took her daughter inside to clean her up.

"I think you're in enough pain, so I'm not going to punish you," she said. "However, Dot, I hope you'll think about this next time you decide to cut practice."

Edna took Dot to a dentist when her mouth had healed, and he used strong dental glue to secure the tooth in the gum. This process had to be repeated several times during her school years. Later, when she lived in Brazil, Dot would apply Elmer's glue to the tooth and shove it back into her mouth. She said it was a good reminder to think before acting on her impulses.

CHAPTER TWO

The Early Years

THE STANGS lived on a one-acre plot of land, half of which was a garden with neat rows of spring lettuce and carrots giving way to corn and tomatoes in the summer. In the 1930s, during the Great Depression, many of Dayton's city residents had moved to the countryside, where they hoped to grow enough food to feed their families. The Stangs were some of the lucky ones, although, as Dorothy said, "the garden took a lot of work to keep it going." She didn't seem to mind as long as she could be outdoors.

However, she knew that her mother needed all the help she could get. With nine children in the house and five of them younger than Dorothy, she had to become a caretaker for the younger siblings. Her brother David said she was "tough."

He tells a story about his older sisters sitting in the kitchen one day eating cake. He had already had his portion but wanted more. He was about five years old. Dorothy heard him say, "Mary, d—you, why won't you give me a little more cake? I'll never speak to you again, and the same goes for you, Maggie." Maggie was the nickname for Marguerite.

Maggie boiled. "Oh boy, you are going to get in trouble!"

Dot marched into the kitchen and dragged David off to the bathroom, where she washed his mouth out with a bar of soap. He screamed and then burst into tears.

Dorothy felt sorry for him and softened. She helped him rinse out his mouth, but she finished by saying, "You are never to speak like that to anyone again. Do you understand?"

David nodded. Many years later, he still remembers that scene. However, he also recalls how protective Dot was of the younger Stangs: "We used to go picking fruit at a large local farm during summer vacations. We could hear the truck coming up the road and we scrambled to get our lunches ready and climb on. The truck left at 5 A.M. Tom and I, who are twins, were about five or six at the time, and we were allowed to go. My sister Barb was seven or eight and Dot was about twelve.

"Dot paid great attention to us kids, and when we would go to the creek at lunchtime, she made sure we ate our sandwiches as well as any fruit we wanted from our pickings. Each of us had a hat and lotion and Dot made sure we put them on."

After a quick jump into the creek to cool off under Dot's watchful eye, they would go back to the job. "Picking fruit was a way for Dad to afford an allowance for us," David says. "We would turn in our 'take,' and then on Saturdays we would get some of it back."

Dot's sister Barb adds this story: "There was a saying for children in Shiloh: 'If you don't behave, the rag pickers will steal you away.' People were actually afraid of them." Rag picker was a name — a slur — for poor people who roamed the farmland roads selling used pots and pans, remnants of fabric, and any secondhand thing they could glean to sell. Whole families, with children in tow, traveled, even lived, in horse-drawn carts. The Depression was especially hard on these poor people.

One Saturday morning, Edna found Dorothy slicing freshly baked bread and making piles of sandwiches for the rag pickers. Dorothy told her mother that the children always looked thin and hungry, and that it wasn't right not to feed them. She wasn't afraid of them either. In fact, she told her mother that next week she planned to make them apple pies.

As Barb recalls, "All our mother could say was, 'That's very good of you, Dot.'"

The Stangs had the largest garden in the neighborhood; the family joked that Henry would turn all of the grass on the property into one garden if he could. He loved the feel of the earth in his hands; the soil was dark and fertile.

He made his own compost from vegetable peelings and horse manure and spread it on the field in the spring. No chemicals or pesticides ever touched his land. The kids said the compost made the weeds grow too fast. He chuckled and said that it was the reason they had so many vegetables. Besides, the vegetables were a great help in feeding a large family.

They all took turns working in the garden, but no one liked helping him more than Dot. He showed all of his children how to smell the dirt and see its richness. Dot's sister Barb remembers "When it rained in summer, the kids would run to take wooden crates and sit out in the garden and breathe in the scent of the good earth as it 'grew.'"

Sometimes Henry went along with a bunch of children to the stream behind their house. He pulled up weeds and wild shoots and showed them how they could eat watercress, wild parsley, and onion grass. He would turn up leaves and point out little mushrooms growing underneath. Dot discovered she could smoke the tempting tall stems of the cat-o'-nine-tail plants. Henry laughed when he found this out, and then he forbade Dot to smoke any kind of wild plant. "Stick to farming," he told her.

"Dad and Dot had a special relationship," Barb says. "It had a lot to do with our garden and our land."

CHAPTER THREE

The Long Road to Brazil

SO, HOW DID Dorothy wind up a nun in Brazil?

Dot's parents sent their children to Catholic schools. Dot attended Dayton's Julienne High School, which offered students many activities. The Mission Club encouraged students to write letters to orphan children in foreign lands and to support those missions by raising money for them. Mission areas are often on continents like Africa, South America, and Asia. Clergy and laypeople from religious communities in North America and Europe spend time teaching Bible studies, English, and other subjects. They often build schools and churches, work in hospitals, and generally try to improve the lives of those living in poorer, less-developed countries.

When Dot was sixteen, she listened closely to a Sister from a mission in China who spoke at Julienne High about the rewards of her work and life. She and her best friend Joan were enthralled. For an adventure-loving teenage girl in the 1940s who had been raised on a small farm, mission work sounded like a suitable and exotic career. She would have the opportunity to travel to faraway places and work in a helping profession, like teaching or nursing.

Shortly after this presentation, Joan took Dot aside. "I've decided to become a Sister of Notre Dame de Namur," she said. "Once I am fully professed — a qualified Sister — I'll teach in a city in the United States and then go to a mission post."

Dot listened to Joan and then said, "You don't think you are going to leave me behind do you? I'm going with you. I can fin-

Dorothy in high school, Dayton Ohio

ish high school in my first year in the convent. I am sure my parents will agree."

Becoming a nun wasn't an easy career choice. The girls would be required to follow a rigorous seven-year course of instruction. Yet they were determined. Joan and Dot saw these nuns, their high school teachers, as role models who seemed to enjoy life in the community as well as their work: attending to the needs of others.

At the top of her application, Dorothy wrote in bold letters: "I want to work in China — those people need us!"

A portrait of Dot at 16

Her parents and younger sisters and brothers couldn't believe this decision would last, but they thought she should try. "We thought she'd be home by Christmas," her sister Barb says. "She even had a handsome boyfriend! I waited up to see him kiss her when he brought her home from dates."

While joining the convent may seem an unusual career choice to seventeen-year-old girls today, for Joan and Dorothy in the 1940s it was a logical decision. They had family and friends from the neighborhood that had entered the religious life, they were comfortable with the rituals and sacraments of the Church, and they knew the rules and requirements of "convent life."

Some girls felt they had received a "call" from God to serve Him. Others were motivated by their teachers, who were good-hearted, smart, and lively; the girls wanted to be like them.

Dot's sister Maggie put it this way:

Dot seemed to know her mind. Despite her full social life and her love of excitement, I think she always had a deep feeling that this might be the right way for her to live her life. She always wanted to help people who were poor and she could serve the Lord at the same time. She also had a deep sense of injustice from an early age. When we were both working at a local pharmacy, we were assigned to the basement to wash out bottles for refills. Dot grumbled because she wanted to work on the cash register upstairs but, despite her pestering, the pharmacist never promoted her. He gave the job to a young man with less experience. I guess she learned, early, that life was not always fair to women . . . even capable ones. She also had that longing for adventure, and in her day, with our family background, entering a missionary order was one very acceptable way to fill that desire.

In 1951, as a full-fledged Sister and a high school graduate, Dorothy went to work in a school in Chicago as an assistant teacher, and her friend Joan went to Columbus, Ohio to teach. These Sisters would earn college and graduate degrees in the years ahead. As friends, however, they did not know when or if they would meet up again.

In 1953 Dorothy left Chicago for a new job. She hoped to be sent to China, but all foreign missionaries had been expelled — the nation was going through political turmoil. She was disappointed, but she was happy to travel and accepted a new mission in Arizona — about 1,500 miles away from Dayton.

CHAPTER FOUR

Arizona, Mission Territory

DOROTHY WAS twenty-two years old when she and two other Sisters arrived in Sunnyslope, a suburb of Phoenix, Arizona. Arizona was still new, having become the forty-eighth state admitted to the United States in 1912. Sunnyslope was considered "mission territory," with no schools or churches for miles around. The area was growing, and three Sisters from Ohio and two Priests from Ireland had volunteered to build a church and school and to teach there.

The students loved Dorothy. In addition to teaching third grade at Holy Trinity School, she played softball with the girls and coached boys' football, all the time wearing the traditional nun's habit of a long black or grey dress topped off with a veil on her head. Students on the sidelines giggled and hoped someone would knock off Sister Dorothy's veil. If somebody did, she would just laugh and clamp it back on her head.

She taught them how to play fair and square. Some boys questioned how much she really knew about football. "I had four brothers," she shouted. "I know the game."

On one occasion, she took her class outside to study because it was so hot in the school. She stood up to teach and forgot that there was an irrigation ditch behind her. She fell in, then started laughing. Without missing a beat she yelled, "This feels great!" Soon, the whole class jumped in.

Dorothy was particularly happy working with the migrant families who had come to Sunnyslope to pick lettuce and grapefruit on the farms. These migrant workers — Spanish-speaking

Sister Mary Joachim, Dorothy's chosen
name when she entered the convent

people from Mexico — traveled from farm to farm in the United
States to help harvest crops. There was a camp nearby, set up
by the owner of a large local farm, where Mexican workers
lived. Many of the children attended the school where Dorothy
taught.

On Fridays after school she and another sister would head
out to teach religion to the children of migrants in the camp's
dining hall. The nuns would drive the children to class by truck
or in their station wagon, picking up stragglers along the way.
One day, while waiting for the class to begin, Dorothy saw three
girls, all about ten years old, huddled over a comic book. She
asked to see it.

Dorothy looked at the image of a browbeaten woman sur-
rounded by dirty dishes and laundry; her face grew serious.

One girl said, "Oh, it's just a cartoon about housework and women — the way we're all going to end up." The girls giggled. "Not if I can help it," Dorothy said. She asked the girls to sit down, and she began to talk about the negative ways women were represented in magazines and about the importance of having self-respect.

CHAPTER FIVE

A Lesson in the Field

THERE ARE many stories of Dorothy's thoughtful caring for all parish members, both the migrants and the local residents. She organized clothing drives where migrants could buy items they needed for fifty cents a bag. She invited everyone in the community to come to pizza parties at the church in the hope that they would get to know each other.

She also noticed that some migrant children had birth defects and she thought she knew why.

On a Friday after religion class, a student of Dorothy's from the migrant camp asked her to meet her parents, who were cutting rows of lettuce in a nearby field. When Dorothy arrived in her old station wagon accompanied by her student, she approached the family, pulled up her skirt, and knelt in the dirt to help with the harvest.

The family smiled and seemed a bit embarrassed. The daughter explained that Sister Dorothy's father had been a farmer, and she knew how to work in the field.

Soon, Dorothy stood up. "Listen, I think I hear a plane. Do you hear it?" She pointed to a speck in the sky. The parents looked up and nodded. "That's a crop-dusting plane," she said. "Let's go over to my car and get in until it passes."

The family continued working. Dot persisted; she had noticed that the mother was pregnant. "The crop-dusting chemicals are unhealthy, especially for unborn children," she said in broken Spanish.

Preparing for Christmas
in Sunnyslope, Arizona

"Please Mami, let's go," said Dorothy's student, and they did.

The seven people wedged into the car and watched as the dust collected on the window. Dorothy spoke, saying that she had noticed a few students in the school with deformed fingers or dark birthmarks on their faces and arms. She remembered her father explaining that certain pesticides sprayed on crops could harm birds and insects, and if it was bad for them it was probably bad for humans too.

"We are all God's children," Dorothy said "You and me. And while we are waiting for our government to outlaw pesticides that can harm us, we have to stand up for ourselves."

In 1963 Dorothy was made principal of the Holy Trinity School. She had many friends in this suburb of Phoenix, and they wanted her to stay forever. She loved the desert, and she used to say, "Oh, you know, I will be buried here under the biggest Saguaro cactus you can find."

But in 1966, Dorothy heard about an opportunity in another mission post: Brazil, South America.

It would be hard for her to leave Arizona. But she believed it was time to live out her faith with a more demanding assignment. The people she would teach were poorer in Brazil, and many were victims of a society that had no regard for its peasants. Most peasants were illiterate and in need of education and support.

Brazil was where she believed she should be. "It might be almost as exciting as going to China," she mused.

PART TWO

First Stop in Brazil, 1966–1974

CHAPTER SIX

Training in Petropolis

DOROTHY's journey to Brazil began in the summer of 1966 when she returned to her home base in Cincinnati, Ohio. The Provincial home of the Sisters of Notre Dame de Namur sat high on a hill overlooking the city. Rushing down a hall, late for lunch, Dorothy ran into her best friend from high school, Joan, who had also signed up for this adventure.

Wow — a different post helping the poor *and* a reunion with Joanie. Dorothy was elated. The two Sisters agreed: "This is almost too good to be true!"

In 1961 the Roman Catholic Pope, John XXIII, began to recruit Sisters and Priests from the United States and Europe to go to Latin America to strengthen the Church. They were to educate baptized Christians about their religion and, through Bible stories and discussions, help the peasants develop a belief in their own human rights. These volunteers would build "Base Christian Communities," communities to give peasants faith in God and in themselves.

All the Sisters were excited, even though they admitted they knew very little about Brazil or the rest of Latin America. An almanac told them Brazil was as large as the United States in square miles. From north to south, the country spans 2,700 miles and is the same distance across at its widest point. It is the largest country in South America and the fifth largest in the world.

In September, 1966, Dorothy and four other Sisters flew to

Rio de Janeiro, a coastal state in southern Brazil. After touching down, they boarded a bus to the hill town of Petropolis, a summer resort and the site of the Catholic University.

Petropolis is a Greek word meaning "City of Peters." Portuguese explorers had been the first Europeans to discover and claim Brazil for the Empire of Portugal. The rulers at that time were Peters I and II. As a result, Portuguese is the country's language, not the Spanish that is spoken in other Latin American countries or by the migrants in Arizona.

After four months of training and studying basic Portuguese, Dorothy and the other Sisters would go north to a small city called Coroatá, in the State of Maranhão, about 1,500 miles from Rio. Joan tells of a visit to a Brazilian family during these first four months: "We were served something unfamiliar to us. It looked a bit like cottage cheese. Wanting to be polite, we ate a full bowl of this new food. Then the host asked, in Portuguese, if we would like another serving. Neither of us had mastered the language yet, but I knew enough to quickly say 'No thank you,' but Dorothy smiled and said, 'Yes, please.'"

Joan tried to signal to Dorothy that she was accepting another bowl of this unusual-tasting food, but Dorothy hadn't understood and forced herself to choke down another bowl. After that, she realized she had to study Portuguese even harder.

About sixty Priests and Sisters were lodged at the Catholic University. In addition to language classes, they were taught about the Brazilian political, educational, and cultural environment. The professor explained that "the people are varied in skin tone and features. They are descended from European adventurers, explorers and rulers, and from African slaves. The Portuguese, Dutch, French and Italians, and even German farmers are part of the history of Brazil." Dorothy was especially happy that her German farm heritage was represented.

Catholic Church in Ouro Preto, Minas Gerais, Brazil

The professor also talked about the state of the Catholic Church in Brazilian society. While Brazilians are very diverse, the Brazilian class system in the 1960s was rigid. The churches reinforced the story of service to the rich: ceilings were lined in gold leaf and furnished with brilliantly painted statues. If peasants attended Mass, they were to stand out of sight in balconies or in dark corners of the church.

Dorothy was astonished by this unfair social structure, and she was even more stunned and troubled by the wretched poverty she saw in the cities. Water with sewage ran freely in the streets, and garbage lay strewn about in broken bags that skinny dogs had chewed open. The experience was nothing like she had ever known. Men and women begged for food, and children commonly slept under a bridge with — and often without — a parent. Their clothing was torn, and they all looked hungry. There was no paid work for these families.

Barbara English, a nun and one of Dorothy's colleagues, described the situation: "There is a wide margin between the rich and the poor, with a long time before the middle class will ever grow. This will take years."

Dorothy wrote to her Sisters in Ohio, telling them that "there is still so much to learn here; however, I am very eager to get to our mission . . . in the North."

A day trip into the mountains established Dorothy as an organizer of adventure and entertainment. One of the French Priests, whom Dorothy had befriended, teased, "They have planned a hike into the mountains for tomorrow, but how can you climb in those outfits?"

Dorothy smiled and said, "You will be surprised, Father Henri. We will do just fine."

In Petropolis, Dorothy, Joan, and the other Sisters of their order wore heavy black wool habits. Each habit was made of six yards of cloth. No matter what size a Sister was, whether plump or thin, her habit was made with those six yards. A black veil covered the Sisters' heads. A wimple — a wide, white collar — and a long, large-beaded rosary completed the outfit.

These habits were made for cooler weather, not for the scorching sun of Brazil. They were also for a different time in history, when Sisters spent a lot of time teaching in classrooms or saying prayers in chapel rather than picking their way through dirty city streets, visiting the poor, or going mountain climbing! Father Henri had a good point.

The night before the climb, Dorothy showed the Sisters how they could tie up their skirts so they would not trip — something she had learned playing football in Arizona. She took a piece of cord, raised the skirt about six inches to mid-calf length, and tied the cord tightly around her waist like a belt. Then she would pull the skirt's fabric over the "belt" to shorten the skirt. She had brought clothesline rope with her, and now she shared it with the others.

Sisters in Brazil, clockwise, from left, Joan Krimm, Marie Heinz,
Dorothy Stang, Patricia MacWade, and Barbara English

What she couldn't teach them was how to scamper down a
rocky hill and keep up with the Priests the way she did. One
Sister went downhill, carefully, on her bottom; another ripped
her skirt; and still others needed the helping hand of a Priest. It
was time for a new style of habit.

The change in clothing was huge and symbolic for the Sisters.
They had been covered from head to toe for years. Now they
were performing new tasks and activities out in the world, in a
different climate in a foreign country. The old way of dressing
did not serve them well. A new, more informal dress code would
not only be more appropriate for their work; it would also remove a barrier between them and the people whom they met.

The Sisters had been discussing a change for months, and
this trek into the hills inspired them to act. Off they went to a
market to buy cloth; they then sewed white blouses and gray,

just-below-knee-length skirts. They also made short white veils for their heads. These new "habits" were cooler and much more comfortable, making movement much easier.

Indeed, the 1960s brought tumultuous change for many religious orders around the world. Not every Sister was comfortable with the new style of dress. For Dorothy and her Sisters, the problem was that the Provincial, the leader of the community in Ohio, had neither been informed of the Brazil Sisters' change of habit nor been asked for her approval. Dorothy worried about this on the way to northern Brazil and wrote to her Superior, "Please, just let us know that this is fine with you, we would like to hear what you think."

They never did hear from her, and they understood her silence to be approval.

CHAPTER SEVEN

Coroatá in the State of Maranhão

THE JEEP bounced along a red dirt road lined with bushes and canopies of tall trees. It carried Sisters Dorothy, Joan, Barbara, and two others, along with their skillful eighteen-year-old Brazilian driver, Braga. Dorothy shouted, "Look at the size of these trees!"

"Mango and Babaçu, Sister," Braga replied, pointing. "That one is about as high as a five-story building. Look Sister, over in that clearing."

"Oh, little goats . . . how dear they are. . . . They're babies!" Dorothy said.

Suddenly, a large black-and-yellow bird streaked across their path; he spread his wings and soared high up into the forest.

Dorothy thought of her family so far away. Her dad would love this forest. It was so green, so beautiful, and so different from the farm in Ohio. Soon after coming to this magical place, she wrote to an Ohio Sister and described the first days in their new town of Coroatá.

We arrived here [in Coroatá] on the 26th of December . . . after spending 2 ½ days in Rosario with other Sisters who had been working there for five years. We spent a wonderful Christmas with them and had our first opportunity to sleep under mosquito nets with bats flying above. They put plastic over the netting to avoid any deposits from the bats. Was great! We learned much. We came here, to our new home. The distance is 125 kilometers, or about 75 miles from Rosario. This took 5 ½ hours to get here. . . . Yes, we really are a bit in the interior.

In fact, as Dorothy's friend Joan tells it, the trip took somewhat longer than Dorothy's exuberant tale would have us believe. "The day was dry," Joan says, "but it was the rainy season. The 'highway' was an unpaved dirt road. Braga had to drive through pond-sized puddles, putting the right-side wheels of the jeep up on the dry bank and crossing slowly through the muddy water. He was never quite sure how deep the puddle was." The tilting passengers held on and laughed nervously.

Then there was the traffic: a herd of sheep bleated and crowded together in the jeep's path. Braga, with Dorothy's help, shooed them to the side of the road. The sheep took their time.

Back in the jeep, they went only a mile or so before Braga announced, "A flat tire, Sisters, I am sorry. I can fix it quickly." Braga was fast at repairing tires, which proved to be a good thing: there was another flat half an hour later. Clearly, life in Brazil was going to be full of surprises and hurdles — more than they had expected.

When they finally entered the town, they pulled up outside a whitewashed house.

"Welcome, Sisters, welcome!" Two young Italian Priests came out to meet the women. "I am Father Laurenço and this is Father Gabriel." The Priests shook hands with all five sisters and never mentioned the way the nuns were dressed. After a light meal, Father Laurenço took them down the street to their own new home. He told them that, for the next two days, they could get acquainted with the town.

Dorothy wrote to her family:

Our house is a converted warehouse but really quite lovely. They did a nice job of getting it ready for us. We have had

A donkey cart waits outside the Sisters' house.

visitors all day long...as well as workmen. All work is hard work — no modern tools — real interesting. Workers wear just trunks, bathing suits, as it is hot for working. Visitors include pigs — they keep our "streets" clear of garbage. Oxen and donkeys are the main form of transportation. Some have horses.... Our town has 8 trucks so it isn't too small.

Coroatá had about 12,000 residents, mostly poor people living in small houses and huts. When they were employed, peasants worked either outside the town on large farms, or "fazendas," or in rice-processing plants, the largest employers in Coroatá. There were also dairy farms in the area that kept herds of milk cows. A tire and truck-repair store, a few roadside stands, and one-room markets completed the economic picture.

Dorothy described the interior of the Sisters' new home to

her family: "We have a butane stove and a refrigerator run by kerosene — very good — a treadle sewing machine, electricity from 6:00 P.M. to 11:00 at night, water from early morning to 7:00 P.M. — or sometimes even later. Not bad. No hot water but it is easily heated on the butane stove. We have beds ... but all here use hammocks to sleep in and we, too, found them most comfortable. You don't sleep in them lengthwise but across the width."

As Dorothy went to sleep that first night, she drifted off dreaming of the green forest, the sheep, and flat tires.

The adventure had begun.

CHAPTER EIGHT

A Young Teacher
Educates the Sisters

THREE DAYS after Dorothy arrived in Coroatá, there was a celebration that she described in a letter. "We had a grand reception into the parish," she wrote. "The bishop came from the capitol. Can't tell you how wonderful he is."

This friendly man was dressed informally for travel in a white short-sleeved shirt and black trousers. After introductions, he admired the nuns' new outfits. He smiled broadly as he told them their habits were "perfect for the situation here . . . simple and practical."

The Bishop told the Sisters that they need not cover their heads either; the congregation would feel more comfortable to see the nuns as real people. Besides, he had a problem with head coverings.

"Some peasants do not come to church because they don't own any scarves," he said. "Others think that they have to cover their heads so they crowd together under one large table cloth to receive communion at the altar rail." Dorothy smiled. He wanted that silly practice to stop. He told the Sisters to put away their veils.

Dorothy wrote: "At the Mass the bishop told the people, in simple words, that we had come to be witnesses of Christ in their midst. He drew a parallel between us coming to Brazil and the coming of Christ to Bethlehem. After the Mass each of us was called up to the altar and presented over the microphone.

Our church is large — it holds 1,000 people standing, without benches."

The Bishop explained to the crowd that Dorothy and her Sisters would lend a hand to the Priests with baptisms and marriages and make home visits to counsel people who needed help. They would also provide religious education for children and adults.

The morning after the reception, Joan and Dorothy were having coffee in their new home. Joan was deep in thought and said little.

"What's wrong?" Dot asked. "You look worried."

Joan nodded. "More like thoughtful." She had met a young woman on her walk home from church, a teacher named Gracinha. Gracinha told Joan she didn't usually go to church, but she came because she was curious. She had never seen American Sisters in Coroatá before this.

Boldly, she told Joan that she felt the people had no faith and that the Sisters' task was impossible.

Dorothy asked, "What did she mean, exactly?"

"That the people don't really care about their religion," Joan said.

"They show up," Dorothy protested. "I'm told the church is usually full. Even those who live in the nearby forest areas come to town and sleep at friends' homes, or in the gardens on mats."

Gracinha had explained to Joan that although all people were baptized in the Catholic Church, there was no religious teaching for peasants after that. They were never taught the basics of their faith. Religious education was reserved for the affluent in Brazil.

Dorothy knew that the peasants were seriously uneducated. She understood Gracinha's point. How much could they really know of their faith?

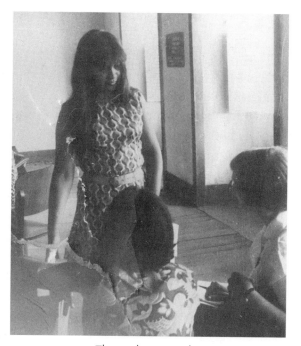

The teacher, Gracinha

Joan said, "I am not quite sure how we should go about this work. It's troubling to think a smart young woman believes our task is hopeless."

Soon after this conversation, Dorothy and Joan saw Gracinha in the marketplace. They invited her home and sat with her in their kitchen.

"Sisters, there is more to this problem," Gracinha said. "For example, there is a rich landowner who goes to church every Sunday with his fifteen-year-old daughter and his wife. During the week he jabs at the workers on his farm with a rifle when he finds them taking a break and he cuts their pay for that day. They are terrified. Other workers have disappeared forever when they were found to have taken food from his kitchen."

Gracinha continued, raising her voice in frustration. "He is typical! He doesn't treat his workers fairly, but we know he gave his daughter a birthday party which cost more than $1,000. Do you understand? We do not belong in the same church! How can we pray next to these people and believe that ours is the same God? It is impossible."

Dorothy sat for a moment in silence. Gracinha's eyes began to water and Dorothy took her hand and patted it, offering a handkerchief. Gracinha dabbed at her tears, then she stood and shrugged. She mumbled that she had a lesson to prepare. Joan gave her a little hug and they thanked her for telling the story and said they would try to help. She shrugged again and left.

The next Sunday, as they walked back from Mass, Dorothy and Joan met a well-dressed landowner and his family. He stopped and smiled, his gold tooth showing. He introduced himself and his family.

Gracinha, who was walking with the Sisters, ignored him and walked on.

CHAPTER NINE

Teaching the People

WHEN DOROTHY arrived in Coroatá, 80 percent of the peasants were Catholics. In the course of training them, she learned the appeal that simple Bible stories held. Telling Bible stories formed the basis of community building, but first the Sisters needed to catch peoples' attention. Brazil is known for parades with lively music and singing, so the nuns and the Priests formed a small procession and walked slowly through the town to a drummer's beat. All it seemed to take were a few recruits singing familiar tunes to encourage others to join in.

The marchers wound through neighborhoods and formed a circle in front of the church. More people came to stand around to see what was happening. Dorothy and her Sisters were making a positive impression and attracting the townspeople.

In his best dramatic tones, the Priest read a Gospel story while Dorothy scanned the crowd. She was looking for men as well as women to become community leaders. Typically, men in Brazil did not attend church; most of them considered it to be a woman's role. Dorothy thought that if she could just find a few men to be leaders, she could build communities more quickly.

She smiled at a man standing nearby. She was proud of her Portuguese and said, "We need you to reach out to your friends who want to make a better life." One or two smiled back and agreed to help plan the next town-square service. "Bring your problems to our meeting," she said, "and we will share them and try to find a way out."

Dorothy and the other Sisters taught religion in Coroatá's six schools. They stuck to the lessons at first and did not pry into the children's personal lives. However, Dorothy could not help herself when she saw that the children were barefoot and wore the same clothes to school day after day.

"Where are your shoes?" she asked.

"Sister, we have no shoes," was the usual answer.

On rainy days, many children were absent. If their clothes were wet, they had nothing to change into. When rains drenched the town, the children were kept home from school. Dorothy wrote to her brothers and sisters and to the Ohio mission office and asked for donations of clothing to be sent as soon as possible. When the boxes of used clothing arrived from America, the children thought she was a saint.

Dorothy listened carefully to the children, who told of their families and their work — or the lack of it.

Inês, age ten with big sad eyes, told Dorothy: "My father stopped working last year. He worked at the rice plant. But now, he has gone away." She said no more.

Tiny eleven-year-old Hector whispered, "Sometimes my mother and I and my brother eat only once a day. Mamae cannot buy enough food for us all and we don't have land to grow corn. Mamae gives the dinner to Papai — she says he has to eat because he carries heavy sacks of rice all day. I am hungry today." After school, Dorothy gave him the snack she had prepared for herself.

Joana, a dark beauty with curly hair, couldn't stop scratching at her arms. "My grandmother came to live with us," she said. "I gave her my hammock because she is very sick. Now I sleep on the floor — bugs bite me."

Dorothy's heart broke for these children and their families. She found a hammock for Joana and negotiated a plot of land in the community garden for Hector and his family so they could grow a few crops. But all the nuns were stumped by Inês's situation. How did her father disappear? No one seemed to know.

The children loved the Bible story about baby Moses, who was found in the bulrushes and grew to be a great leader. They understood that, like the Israelites, their families might be able to find their own land. Soon parents began turning up to hear Dorothy's lessons. Eventually they began to share their life stories with her.

There was no end to the hardships: worn-out soil conditions meant sparse crops and not enough food to eat; a rice-processing plant had closed and put people out of work; they could not read, yet some wanted to go to school; babies and children needed care that parents did not know how to give.

One parent, Cristina, explained her situation. "I have four children," she said. "I work from seven in the morning until seven at night, cook, clean, everything. My husband is out of work." Her only pay was the leftover food she was given some evenings. Her boss felt he did enough by paying for medical care when her family needed it.

At a home visit, Dorothy and Joan persuaded the employer's wife that Christina's self-esteem and work habits would be better if she were paid. The wife admitted that she had considered paying her with money; she just had to figure out how to hide the fact from her husband.

The Sisters were happy with the outcome of this meeting. They knew, however, that as they went through neighborhoods and brought about change, they would not always be welcome in the richer, more established sections of town.

Peasant families, on the other hand, took delight in the home visits of the Sisters. The custom was to clap, two or three times, at the entrance of the hut to announce their presence outside. Invited in, the nuns played with the children and asked the adults to come to church or to a meeting in the square.

Dorothy was scheduled to call on some prostitutes who lived in her district. In a street made up of little more than one-room shacks with a bed and a chair, she heard the women's sad stories: mistreatment, a false marriage promise, and abandonment by customers.

One woman told Dorothy, "We have no other way to earn money; I have two children to feed." Dorothy just listened.

The next time she came to the neighborhood, the same woman grabbed the nun and gave her a big hug. Dorothy wrote home: "I thought my ribs would break she was so glad to see me again. I pray for her and her friends and I think about how to help them improve their lives."

CHAPTER TEN

Out from Coroatá

HOME VISITS to rural settlers were an even greater challenge; at least 70,000 people lived in the forest, nearly six times the population of Coroatá. Some villages were large but many were small, with only six or seven huts clustered together. Still other families lived alone in isolated spots on wooded trails with neighbors more than a mile away. Dorothy and her group were expected to visit little villages and outposts at least once a year, and she loved these visits the best, even though travel was complicated.

She described one journey to a large village in the spring of her first year. Dorothy, another Sister, and a Priest "went by train and then . . . after quite a walk, we reached the river, where we took a canoe to the other side where most of the people live." Here, in a large village, a local farmer provided room for them to stay.

> We came home by trolley. This is a small board, a yard square that has train wheels. It runs along a track when pushed by two men or boys, who stand on the board and, with long poles, push against the railroad ties. Father and the two of us sat on the front of the board, our feet dangling over the tracks! The distance covered was only 18 miles but the trip took three hours! It poured rain most of the time, and even though we had raincoats, we looked like drenched rats when we reached Coroatá!

Typically, whether their destination was near or far, two Sisters went along with a Priest to a ranch or farm, where the owner,

Transportation for Dorothy with friends

his family, and his workers came together for Mass. Early one Sunday morning, with high humidity and a soft drizzle falling, Dorothy and Joan drove with Father Gabriel to a "fazenda," a large farm. When they arrived, they saw that the altar had been set up outdoors in the front yard of a large home; the altar was covered by a tarp strung up on four poles to keep off any rain.

Senhor Mendonça and his wife, dressed in their Sunday best, came out to greet them. They shook hands and explained to the Sisters, "The people come here from the forest, but they are often late; we can start when you wish."

"Let us wait a little while," said the Priest.

The farmer invited them into his house. He led them through a cool, large living room to a porch at the back of the ranch. Stepping out onto the grass, they looked at fields that stretched as far as the eye could see. Off in the distance, trees appeared to be the size of toys.

"Rice, my friends," said Senhor Mendonça. "It is what all of

Latin America eats." They admired the furrowed fields. Dorothy thought of her own small family farm in Ohio; she could see how Senhor Mendonça had come to his wealth.

A little boy dressed in a perfectly starched white shirt and navy shorts came out to say that many people were waiting. His father, the farmer, scooped him up in his arms. Dorothy suddenly thought of little Hector; this farmer's son would never know the pain of hunger.

The Priest looked at his watch and announced that he could begin the Mass. About sixty people attended. Many of them were employed by this landowner and either carried water for irrigation or harvested rice in the fields — backbreaking work. The Priest gave a sermon, baptized newborn children, and performed two weddings.

While Dorothy assisted at the Mass, she noticed that only a few peasants said the prayers or sang the hymns. And when the service was over, the men and women did not stop to speak with Senhor Mendonça. Dorothy and Joan tried to mix with the crowd and greet the families; they admired the babies and introduced themselves. Some peasants smiled shyly in return but said little.

After a grand Sunday dinner of pork, chicken, rice and beans, coffee, beer, and dessert, Senhor Mendonça invited the Priest and the Sisters to spend the night. They all declined, saying the trip home was not that long. On the way back, Dorothy asked Joan, "Do you think they don't respond because they are shy, or they don't understand my Portuguese? Maybe it's because we are new? Or is there something else?"

Joan just shook her head. "I am not sure."

When a village was farther from town, they had no choice but to stay overnight with the ranch owner. The Sisters felt increasingly uneasy with this tradition. The year had flown by since they arrived in Coroatá, and Dorothy and her Sisters had heard and seen peasant life firsthand. They suspected that they could no longer accept the landowners' hospitality.

The peasants saw these large farm owners as the enemy, and indeed, some were. Certain farmers paid the peasants very little and could be harsh masters. Low or no pay meant the peasants were like slaves with no way out of their oppression.

Dorothy remembered Gracinha's words: "We do not belong in the same church! How can we pray next to these people and believe that ours is the same God? It is impossible."

"We can't remain in the comfortable old ways," Joan said, "ministering mainly to the literate and affluent. We came here to work with the poor."

Dorothy agreed. "In order to win the trust of the peasants," she said, "we will have to eat what they eat and live like they live."

All the Sisters agreed: they had to break with the landowners in order to win the peasants' trust. Once they had this trust, the nuns hoped they would be able to teach the peasants about their faith and build up their sense of self-worth.

CHAPTER ELEVEN

Word Gets Around

IN 1962 Pope John XXIII wanted to "open the window to let in a fresh breeze," and he called the Second Vatican Council in Rome to bring the Catholic Church up-to-date. He and other clergy wanted to make Catholicism more democratic and less a rich people's religion. Many changes were inevitable. The nuns' black habit, for example, was no longer obligatory. The Church also did away with mandatory Latin Mass and required that the liturgy be said in a country's native language, which was called the vernacular.

Now, in the mid-1960s, clergy members were encouraged to form and lead small community meetings of peasants to strengthen their faith. The rural peasants, in particular, loved these gatherings; they had lived for a long time in isolation and had not known such friendly church people.

How did Dorothy carry on these meetings? When she had assembled a little group — a future church community — they held a Mass (if a Priest was present) or a prayer service in Portuguese. In simple language and with great energy, Dorothy would explain the essence of the day's scripture. The people caught on and began to see the meaning of the message for their own lives.

As in the town, Dorothy began to look for natural leaders in the forest villages to continue her work when the Priest and the Sisters could not be there. Community leaders read or told a Gospel story, spoke about the problems of the day, and began to form support systems.

These local men and women took their jobs very seriously. Some men bought black cloth and asked their wives to sew long, dress-like "cassocks" for them. These were the cloaks the Priests often wore when they visited peasants' homes. The men thought the community would listen to them more closely if they dressed like Priests.

The Sisters chuckled about this in private, but they had to put an end to this practice. "I am sorry, Carlos," Dorothy explained to a villager. "To be a Priest takes several years of study. Only then can one wear this costume!"

As a substitute for wearing the black robe, the Sisters introduced each leader at every meeting and chose him to read the Gospel or to give a special talk. In this way, they celebrated every person who stepped up to the job of community building.

Dorothy's own appearance had become more like that of the people. She wore a T-shirt, a short skirt or long shorts, and sandals, and she carried a cloth or plastic bag with papers and her Bible. She was a welcome figure traveling the dirt roads around Coroatá. She loved her work and was out in the forest more than she was in town. She helped to build more and more communities.

In one area, 600 people showed up to meet Dorothy when they heard she and a Priest were making a visit. When she had first come to that place seven months before, only fifty people had come for the Mass.

Word of her work traveled. In 1964 the Brazilian government which had enjoyed a period of democracy, was taken over by the military, and it presided over the country until the early 1980s. A few officers were stationed in Coroatá, supposedly to keep the peace. In truth, they were there to watch the Priests and Sisters, who were gaining popularity with the peasants. A seemingly friendly lieutenant brought the Sisters a gift now and then, the English edition of *Time* magazine. It was a way for him to visit their home, to meet the nuns, and try to discover what, exactly, the Sisters were doing.

The new religious approach — forming base Christian communities of peasants and rural farmers — combined with the popularity of the Communist Party in Brazil worried the military government. Communism as a political system had taken hold in Cuba in 1960 and overthrown the government. Idealistic Brazilian Communists wanted more power for the people. These young intellectuals, professionals, and labor leaders had fought a short, bloody war with the military on the border of Bolivia and Brazil, and they were crushed by the army.

In the late 1960s, when the lieutenant was visiting the nuns, he and his commanding officer suspected that the Sisters might be sympathizing or collaborating with Communists. He asked many questions.

"We can do the same thing," Dorothy said to her Sisters. They began to ask the lieutenant questions about how many officers were in Coroatá, what their mission was, and how they spent their days. For some time, both sides played this game of "cat and mouse."

Then, on one visit, a torn page from a military manual fluttered from the magazine. Dorothy picked it up from the floor. It showed lethal-looking knives and guns. The lieutenant muttered, "I had to use these weapons in a battle with young revolutionaries over the border of Brazil." He shook his head. "I hope that we will never have to use these in Brazil again."

The Sisters looked at him curiously and nodded in sober agreement. When he had left, they laughed at his attempt to scare them. He seemed to say, "Don't stir up the peasants or you might be punished." Dorothy refused to be frightened. "I'd say we must be doing something right!" she exclaimed. "The military is actually threatened by the words of the Gospel."

PART THREE

Southeastern Pará, Brazil, 1974–1982

CHAPTER TWELVE

Moving to the "Wild West" of Brazil

ONE MORNING, Joan said to Dorothy, "Did you see Cristina and her children outside whitewashing their little house and planting flowers? I think the family is a little better off now."

Dorothy smiled. "I guess we started a trend." Dorothy always planted flowers or fruit trees whenever she made a home for herself. A few families were doing the same.

However, there were still many peasants out of work and the odds of finding a job were slight.

"These people are desperate for a change, even if it means moving far away. What are we to do?" Dorothy sighed.

In 1972 there were vast numbers of people living in poverty in Brazil, not only in Coroatá but also in other small-town slums and in drought areas along the coast. The government seemed to come to their aid, offering plots of land to all Brazilian residents in the neighboring Amazon State of Pará. Road building had begun into the Amazon forest, and this made it easier for settlers to reach the territory. Transportation was provided for anyone who wanted to move there.

Peasants were told that they could become farmers and own their own plots for free. "Land for the people, for the people without land" — that was the slogan for agrarian reform. At the same time, the government thought they could populate the huge and empty rain forest region and relieve some of the cities of slum dwellers. Thousands of poor people chose to go to Pará, the State next to Maranhão.

Dorothy was worried about the welfare of families who wanted to move; she knew they would need to build base communities there. The city poor she knew had few or no skills for living in the forest. In addition, farmers could not grow the same crops they had in other parts of the country because the soil was different. Dorothy pondered this for a short time, and when some families from Coroatá asked her, she agreed to go with them to Pará.

"I kind of knew this was how it might be . . . you would follow them," Joan said.

Dorothy feared for the peasants' safety. Multinational corporations, businessmen, and even Brazilian politicians from the south had been given title to huge tracts of land. Some large landowners did not want settlers on their land, even though the land was empty and uncultivated. There was news that local thugs were hired to push naïve settlers off the land. It was clear that the land-settlement project would grow complicated.

In addition, there were almost no missionaries in Pará where the families would go. Dorothy asked her friend Joan to come along. However, Joan was already running at top speed in Coroatá. She not only taught in the schools and worked with special-needs children, but also she had begun to build a center for teenagers. The local teens often needed advice about their futures, about their families, and about other boys and girls, and Joan had a way with them. The young crowd that was coming to the center increased by the week. Joan felt she could not leave Coroatá.

A new, younger Sister of Notre Dame de Namur, Rebeca Spires, had arrived in Coroatá. Dorothy asked her to come along. Becky was part Native American, facile at learning languages, and eager to get out to the forest where indigenous people lived.

Dorothy needed someone to help her, and Becky was perfect for the job. She agreed to go when Dorothy promised that, eventually, she could work directly with the native Brazilians.

The Bishop in the region of Marabá, which is in Pará, invited Dorothy and Becky to move near a town called Abel Figuereido. After a round of parties and amid prayers and good wishes, they rode off, first traveling by train and then by bus.

"The bus was hot but the sights were magnificent," Becky remembers. "It was more rural than the forest areas around Coroatá. The trees were so green and the vegetation so thick and impenetrable. The forest was still relatively untouched except by a few natives and some poor farmers already living there. We passed only five villages along the entire 130 miles of the red dirt road."

At the border, military guards stopped them and shouted loudly into the bus, "Take your suitcases and your belongings down from the racks. We need to do a search."

Dorothy and Becky got off the bus and offered their few belongings to the men. "What reason have you for entering Pará?" asked an officer. "Do you have papers?"

Dorothy produced the letter inviting them to live and teach in the diocese of Marabá.

"OK," one grumbled. "You can go back on the bus."

He stamped the letter and their passports, and Dorothy and Becky were off again.

CHAPTER THIRTEEN

The New Challenges

"WELCOME, SISTERS," said Dom Estevão. This Bishop, the head of the Marabá Diocese, came out of his house to meet Dorothy and Becky. He took them to meet the local pastor and other missionaries — French Priests who had volunteered to teach religion, reading, and writing to the settlers. The men had prepared a delicious meal of *coq au vin* for the occasion, and they all sat down to eat amid loud conversation, laughter, and a little wine. The Priests were delighted to have help because the diocese was large; they also were happy that they would have company for the occasional card games on Saturday nights.

In general, the church supported the peasants in the land movement. Based on her experience, Dorothy felt that she and Becky needed to go out to meet the peasants as she had done before. Almost immediately, Dorothy found this work more difficult than it had been in Coroatá. The people there had been gentle and open to the Sisters' teachings. But here, there were cultural differences among the newly settled peasants. Many had been bussed or flown in from far-off states. Some were shy and kept to themselves, refusing outside help even from the Sisters. Others were brash, loud, and aggressive and were quick to start fights with their neighbors.

When she approached the small huts, some of which had no doors, the people hid from the nuns or simply said, "No," they would not come to a meeting. One woman told her, "Sister, we do not go with the people from the other states, they are loud and unkempt; we are a better people."

Dorothy looked at the woman's ragged dress. She smiled but said nothing. She had heard that people from the State of Minas Gerais thought they were superior to others. Other new settlers explained that there was no time for meetings and, anyway, the soldiers had come after them to break up groups larger than two or three persons.

Dorothy told the Priests, "We used to have processions which ended in our town square with a meeting — I even beat my tambourine! But there is no town square here — we're in such a small village. And I don't know how many people would follow us anyway."

The local pastor was a cautious man. "Please, Sisters," he said. "Teach only Bible studies and reading and do not try to get too many to come to class. Eventually they will show up."

The caution was echoed by a young lawyer, a member of the Pastoral Land Commission (CPT). The CPT had been established in 1975 to report harassment and violence against settlers and clergy to the Brazilian authorities. The lawyer sympathized with the difficulty Sister Dorothy was having in building base Christian communities, but he also counseled her to move slowly.

Dorothy never moved slowly, though, and for a while she was discouraged. Continuous objections from the local Priest about her methods and the ever-present military hassles put her off. She prayed and thought, believing that there had to be some other way to reach these peasants.

Becky and Dorothy came up with a new tactic to educate those who did come to religion class. They chose Bible stories that stirred up discussions about farming methods and lumber use, markets for crops, and even ways to transport crops to market.

The parable, or Gospel story, of the mustard seed was a favorite with new settlers. Jesus told the story of a man, a sower,
whose seeds fell in many places, some on poor soil and some on
rocks. But some seeds fell on good ground, where roots could
take hold. The settlers immediately connected this to their experience trying to grow crops on the new, less-fertile land in
Pará. Some said their manioc seeds — a staple when ground
into flour — would not grow in the earth near their huts. Others had found ways to improve the soil so that the seeds would
take root. Bit by bit, the farmers formed connections, and they
created new base communities.

In the midst of this budding success, Dorothy received some
troubling news. She pulled a letter from her pocket that evening
and read it to Becky.

CHAPTER FOURTEEN

A Test of Reality

"IT'S FROM THE new Bishop, Alano," she told the younger Sister. Dorothy began to read, shaking her head in disbelief. "He writes, 'A priest from another church, about 20 miles from here, has filed a complaint with the Army about your way of teaching. He said that you are stirring up the farmers against the government.'" There had even been an accusation that she was "communistic."

Dorothy continued reading. The Bishop apologized for having to ask them to go to a military hearing, but he had to comply with the government's orders. There would be five of them, the Sisters and three Priests. He said he would go with them and prepare them beforehand. When they met, he told them that they only had to answer direct questions. They should keep their answers short and be as positive as possible.

On the day of the hearing, the Bishop accompanied them to meet the inquisitors. The officer in charge spoke to the Bishop: "Your Excellency, you may leave, I know you are a busy man." He refused to leave. He stayed the whole day in an adjoining room while they interrogated Dorothy and the others.

Becky was the first to be called, and her turn was short. "What are you doing here in Pará?" the officer asked. She said that she had come to Pará to teach religion, reading, and writing to the peasants. Though nervous, she answered calmly, and the officer dismissed her quickly.

It was Dorothy he wanted to grill. She watched as he rifled

through a stack of papers. Relief flooded over her when he pulled a single sheet from the pile. He waved it at her.

"You are Sister Dorothy Stang?"

She nodded.

"What *exactly* are you doing here in Pará?"

She explained about the religion and literacy teaching. She kept her answers short and did not mention that she was helping to develop communities or building skills among peasant settlers.

Still, he was not satisfied, and he leaned closer to look her in the eye. "Are you sure you are not teaching the peasants to criticize our government?"

"Yes, I am sure," she answered honestly.

"I understand you bring the farmers together and teach them about farming. What could *you* know about this?"

Dorothy explained that she had grown up on a farm in the state of Ohio in the United States and had worked with her father, who taught her about soil and crops.

With the growl of a man defeated, he warned, "Sister, stick to teaching the peasants their religion if you must, but do not become a political person. We will know if you do this and we will be forced to take further action."

The next day, the Bishop conducted a day of prayer and reflection. He read from a passage in the New Testament and then, in a short homily, assured them that they had done the right thing and that they were doing their work in the spirit of Jesus Christ.

He ended by saying, "Being falsely accused of a crime and having to defend yourselves is part of the struggle you have taken on here in Brazil. It is up to each of you to decide if you can do this work."

CHAPTER FIFTEEN

Friends Go in Different Directions

IT NEVER CROSSED the Sisters' minds to stop their work. They were harassed and wrongly accused of misconduct more than once — they came to see it as just part of the job. The farmers and peasants loved them, and by 1977 Dorothy and Becky had managed to help build nearly thirty communities. By 1979 there were two teams working in the area around the town of Abel Figuereido; some Priests worked with Becky and two Priests worked with Dorothy.

Abel Figuereido was becoming better organized. Becky had been able to follow her true passion and expand her work with the Indian tribes served by the Missionary Indians' Council (CIMI). Dorothy recognized a certain feeling: it was time to go where there were "the poorest of the poor," where there was a greater need for her. Both Sisters made promises to get together as soon as possible, and Becky waved goodbye as Dorothy climbed aboard a run-down bus for the ninety-mile ride to the town of Jacunda.

The bus bumped and trundled along on the dirt roads of the forest. As they left Abel Figuereido, Dorothy saw cut-down trees and smelled the burning forests. And once out of town, as far as the eye could see there were hundreds of deforested acres. It was a shock. Trees had been sheared off right at the ground, and the acrid smell of smoke drifted in through the open windows, stinging her nose and making her eyes water. She felt sad to

Burned and deforested Amazon land

think of all the displaced birds and animals, and she wondered how many had died in the fires. A strong emotion flooded over her; surely it is wrong to destroy creation in this way.

When rich businessmen and politicians took possession of land in the Amazon, they hired local ranchers to help build up their timber businesses. What Dorothy saw was the result of their work — tall trees cut down, raw lumber piled on large trucks to be sold in ports far away, miles of ground cover burned, and fast-growing grass seed springing up through the earth.

When the grass was tall, cowboys herded in long-horned beef cattle to graze. New roads were cut into the forest to enable ranchers to move in their equipment and move their trucks out to markets. Beef brought a good price in Brazil and in global markets.

The government had arranged for peasants to go to the Amazon and told them to farm any land that was not in productive use — in other words, which had no crops growing on it. After five years, the land would be theirs to keep. However, bound-

Cattle graze on recently deforested land

aries between ranchers' and peasants' lands were blurred; few large landowners really knew where their ranches stopped and the peasants' plots of land began. Some did not care. The land-development agencies were understaffed and slow to process paperwork. Most peasants never got proper titles of ownership to their plots.

When Dorothy witnessed the remnants of burned huts along the way, she worried about the peasants; they were such easy prey for violent conflicts. She knew what her job would be: help the poor learn skills to survive and, just maybe, teach them to protect their forest.

CHAPTER SIXTEEN

The Courage to Carry On

IN JACUNDA, one family graciously made room for Dorothy in their little home; two hammock hooks against a wall was all she needed. The family loved having Dorothy there, but it would not be peaceful for long. Jacunda was growing fast, and by the late 1970s, tension was mounting between peasants and large ranch owners. Illegal loggers and cattle ranchers burned peasants' crops in an effort to get them to move, and if they did not move, they burned their homes as well.

In a letter to her Sisters in Ohio, Dorothy explained the situation:

> One evening I was getting ready for bed. It was January 2, 1981, and I was the only one at home. Some farmers knocked loudly at my door. They said, "Sister, our brother José has been murdered right in front of his hut because he stood up to the men who came to burn his home." These men indicated they would return the next day with more farmers because they wanted me to help them figure out what they could do. They . . . began planning . . . a more vigorous means of self-defense. The authorities never protect the settlers . . . [but] the people are becoming stronger.

The farmers had begun to organize legally by forming a labor union. Some union members regularly visited Dorothy's home to strategize and get advice. Dorothy had been somewhat successful in dealing with the National Institute for Colonization and Agrarian Reform (INCRA). It was INCRA that was responsible for keeping track of the land grants. However, in most cases, the local INCRA authorities didn't know who actually owned the land. They were polite to Dorothy, but some saw her as a pest because they could not answer most of her questions.

Military officers watched her house constantly to see which farmers and Priests were coming and going. Dorothy wrote: "In the wee hours of the feast of the Three Kings, January 6, it was decided that I should get out for a few days. I am writing from a bit of a hideaway." Dorothy explained that a new law against foreigners gave officers the right to "get rid of anyone that disturbs the false peace." Had she been caught at home, she would have been blamed for any action that the farmers decided to take and, perhaps, sent back to the United States.

Dorothy returned from her hiding place to find her farmer friends planning to take matters into their own hands — with guns. She tried to convince her people not to do this. "Once you have killed a person, you will never be the same. It affects your spirit and your soul."

Still, she was sympathetic to their strong feelings. There was no one to monitor these huge tracts of land. The illegal ranchers knew they could get away with their crimes. The few local police in an area protected their own jobs and their lives by looking out for the interests of the rich. She wished she could do more, openly, to help her friends.

However, she remembered the words of the pastor in Jacunda who had criticized her most recently: "Don't be in such a hurry to improve these people's lot — they are poor and many are not capable of learning what you teach. Wait for them to ask you for help. Don't push ideas on them."

Dorothy felt that she was at a crossroads. She knew she should obey the pastor's wishes, yet she was disheartened by his words and the restrictions that they put on her work. She believed she was right to continue her work—helping the peasants learn the skills to survive by building communities, churches, and schools. She had to stand up for them.

When Becky came to visit, they compared notes. Becky, too, was confronting large logging businesses which kept pushing the Brazilian Indians deeper into the forest. The indigenous tribes were struggling to hold onto their land.

Alone with her Sister, Dorothy confided, "I have tried to hold back, to avoid counseling the farmers about their rights. But it just seems wrong for me to do that." Dorothy admitted she was stubborn, but she also knew that sometimes that trait gave her strength.

She continued, "I could return to Coroatá or Ohio—there are poor everywhere who can use my skills. But I live here and this is my mission, to be poor with the poor and work with them to make a better life."

She told Becky that at a meeting in Jacunda, she had heard that a new Bishop, Dom Erwin Krautler, might be able to use her in the diocese of Altamira, about 350 miles away on the Xingu River in the Amazon. Bishop Krautler was working with Sisters and Priests to settle poor peasants in his area. He was "shifting the pastoral orientation of his area, toward . . . a preferential option for the poor." In other words, he was teaching his staff of clergy to go out and build communities of faith, rather than having them travel from village to village to say Mass and see the people once a year.

Dorothy wanted to go where she thought she could make the biggest difference, and she thought that Bishop Krautler might be more likely to support her; she knew she could help him. She had already cleared her plan with Bishop Alano, and he agreed that she should go north.

Becky knew how much the people loved Dorothy, but she

had heard criticism of her Sister, too — mainly from the clergy. Dorothy worked too fast, had too many ideas, and was inflexible in her passionate support of the peasants. Becky prayed that her capable and kindhearted friend would be more welcome in Bishop Krautler's large diocese in northern Pará. They both remembered the words the Bishop had said to them after the military hearing: "Go as far as your courage will carry you."

PART FOUR

On the "TA," 1982–2005

CHAPTER SEVENTEEN

Meeting the New Bishop

BISHOP KRAUTLER'S office is located in the colorful and bustling harbor port city of Altamira on the Xingu, the largest of the Amazon tributaries. Its streets teem with people. Boats of all sizes go up and down all day, carrying loads of fresh fish, onions and carrots, oranges and mangoes, and, of course, timber. These river boats glide along to the capital city of Pará, Belém, on the Atlantic Ocean.

Dorothy told her story to the Bishop: it was time for her to move on; her people in the southeast of Pará knew how to build communities. There were also other missionaries there to help. "My start-up work is done," she said.

Bishop Krautler was tall and thin — and relatively young for a Bishop. An Austrian by birth and a Brazilian citizen by choice, he came to the country before entering the priesthood. Now, as the head of the diocese, he had a huge task: helping to settle nearly 100,000 peasants on land along the "TA," the Trans Amazon Highway.

This highway is 3,300 miles long. Only the first 100 miles are paved. It cuts through the Amazon region, although most of it is no more than red dirt framed by trees and bushes with just a few trails leading into the forest. Still, new settlers all shared the same daydream: a better life as Amazon farmers. It would take a long time to realize the dream.

Bishop Krautler told Dorothy that the newcomers, first and foremost, needed a strong faith to inspire them to carry on. They also needed to learn to farm and, eventually, to read and write if they were going to someday rise out of their poverty. He listened carefully to Dorothy.

"Sister Rebeca and I worked in small villages and towns," she explained, "and we helped to build community schools and chapels. We both grew up in rural areas of the United States so it was natural for us to try to help with farming too. Unfortunately, we were somewhat hampered by the local politics." The Bishop suspected that this was an understatement. Dorothy hoped this would not affect his decision.

He knew there had been disagreements between the nun and some of the clergy. Dorothy told him that his predecessor, Bishop Alano, in Jacunda, once so supportive of her, thought it was time for her to move on. Her reputation as a self-starter was not always appreciated. And the military had expelled some Priests in the Bishop's diocese, and others had even been killed — all because of their involvement with the poor farmers. Bishop Alano did not want Sister Dorothy to be next.

Bishop Krautler was impressed with Dorothy's honesty and her courageous and deep commitment to justice. In turn, Dorothy could see how dedicated he was to the cause of these needy landless, and she very much wanted to help.

The Bishop warned her about depending too much on INCRA, the agency in charge of settling the peasants. "They provide food for the settlers for a year and give each family a hoe and a shovel. But the agency is understaffed and unable to do any training or show the peasants where they should build homes."

He paused and dropped his head. "After a year they are supposed to become self-sufficient. . . . I don't know how."

Dorothy smiled and said, "I will help you. Give me the poorest area and I will go there."

He told Dorothy he would give her the most difficult section of the TA east of Altamira; there were only a few trails — not roads — into the forest, and the people were left to find plots of land for themselves. There, she could begin to try and gather the peasants into communities. INCRA had a distribution site for tools and food farther out on that section of the highway. It was called Centro Nazaré; beyond that, there was a small town called Anapu. He told her she could begin her work not far from the edge of Altamira's town and work her way out east. "Just remember," he said, "there are not even signs on the trails into the forest."

"What about big ranches?" Dorothy asked.

"We don't have as many large ranches as you had in Jacunda, but they're coming. . . . The land wars will continue, we can be certain of that."

"I am not afraid," she said.

Bishop Krautler was hopeful, as was Dorothy. He introduced Dorothy to a Priest named Father Lucas. Lucas had already organized seven base communities, and he was very glad to have Dorothy's help.

CHAPTER EIGHTEEN

INCRA's "Best Staff Member"

IN THE LATE 1970S, before Dorothy arrived in Altamira, peasants who had some farming skills and a little education were bussed or flown to this Amazon area west of the city on the TA. Some came from more than 800 miles away.

By early 1982, however, when Dorothy came, INCRA was overwhelmed with the job of resettling the Amazon land. A new crop of peasants had heard that the land there was free, and many arrived on their own. They were told to go east and take some land that was not being farmed productively.

Traveling east was difficult. Crude, narrow roads had been cut into the forest on either side of the TA. Here, the red surface was full of holes and stones. Getting around meant long hours of walking or waiting for a daily bus, which might be late or not come at all.

This was Dorothy's territory.

Bishop Krautler found her a place to stay across the street from his home in Altamira; she boarded with another order of Sisters. At the beginning, she went out for the day with Father Lucas and returned late at night.

One of the first families that Dorothy and Lucas encountered had a small farm by the side of a road close to the TA. Paulo, a young farmer, and his wife, Eliza, stared at Dorothy as she and Lucas introduced themselves. They had never seen a white woman in the forest before. Not only that, but she was traveling

The muddy Trans Amazon Highway in the 1980s

with a Priest, who introduced her as a nun — dressed in a skirt and a T-shirt!

Eliza was preparing the noon meal. A few chickens pecked in the dirt and steam rose from a pot hung over the fire on a metal hook. A skinned squirrel lay on a large leaf, waiting to be grilled. The wife shyly greeted Dorothy and gave her a gentle hug, a typical Brazilian hello. Beyond them, Dorothy could see corn growing and a few rows of other vegetables.

She asked, "Is this the land that INCRA has given you?"

Paulo said, "No," and explained that he had grown up there. A few farm families had settled in the Amazon years before the land reforms. Still, they were rarely visited by missionaries, who preferred to gather people together in village settlements.

Eliza called her daughter over to meet the visitors. She invited them to stay and eat with them, and Dorothy and Father Lucas quickly agreed. They had the same thought as they exchanged glances: *perhaps we can start to build a base community here.*

Dorothy asked Paulo whether he knew if they had any close neighbors. He said that a family had come by, and he had shown them where they could build and plant. She asked if they would like to have a Mass said there in front of their house; they could invite anyone else, including the new neighbors. Paolo shrugged his shoulders, but Eliza said that it might be a good idea. The nun and the Priest made arrangements to come back in a few weeks to say a Mass and baptize any new babies. They hoped they would get enough people to sow the seeds of a small community.

As they walked home, Dorothy and Father Lucas discussed the problem with the "first come first served" policy for the landless. Even though there was much land available, he reminded her that the deeds to the land were hard to get, and when they were given to the peasant families, the boundaries could be wrong or nonexistent.

Some deeds that ranchers held were fakes; these ranchers falsified deeds by putting crickets into a box with a deed. With a little dirt on them — and having been chewed up in part by the crickets — these fake documents were passed off as original deeds to the land occupied by the illegal ranchers.

The two missionaries decided that Sister Dorothy should introduce herself at the INCRA office in Altamira so that when arguments over land arose, she would be able to work with the local INCRA staff to try to get documents.

The next day, Dorothy visited the small office. It was mobbed with landless peasants carrying their few belongings in paper bags and plastic suitcases. A few carried food. The room was hot, and it smelled of bodies that had not been washed in days. It was noisy, too. Everyone was trying to get information, either from each other or from the two counselors who already looked tired at ten o'clock in the morning.

"Where is my plot? Where is my plot?" asked one man to no one in particular.

"Where should I go?" asked another fellow. A man turned to Dorothy. "What do I need to buy while I am in the city? I have some money."

A ragged looking man who stood nearby sidled up to the one with money and said, "I will show you." They began to leave the office.

Dorothy called after the newcomer and warned him to be careful. Peasants were not the only ones looking for a new life; petty criminals and robbers came to the Amazon, as well. Someone "with money" was easy prey for thieves and might never get to farm a piece of land.

An INCRA counselor motioned Dorothy to approach his desk. He moved some papers off a chair and plopped them on the floor next to another pile. He shook her hand and invited her to sit. She explained that, with the approval of Bishop Krautler, she had come to help with the settlement of these new, landless immigrants.

He was astonished. "You will help us?"

"Yes, I will," she said.

His eyes widened when she told of her experiences in Coroatá and southern Pará. She asked if they had a plan to settle the newcomers on the eastern stretch of the TA. He explained that those peasants could go to a place called Nazaré, about fifty miles away. It was a two-day walk, or a one-day bus ride if they could afford it. In Nazaré, they would be given food and some tools and supplies for farming. "That's all we can do," he said.

As Dorothy left, the counselor smiled and shouted after her, "I will tell the State Office in Belém that we have a 'new assistant.'"

Dorothy laughed and thanked him.

She watched as a young woman — the other INCRA counselor

— stood at the door and mopped the perspiration that was running down her face. Over and over again she said, "Go out on the TA highway and walk until there is no one working a plot. You can go down any trail that crosses the highway."

The settlers nodded to her and slowly moved out of the office. Only a few realized that they should ask: "Do I turn right or left?"

CHAPTER NINETEEN

It's All about Land

DOROTHY TRIED to use her motorbike on the TA, but the roads were too rutted for the little bike, and she abandoned it in favor of walking — several miles each day. The sun was hot, the air was humid, and when it rained it poured. She carried a piece of oil cloth, which she pulled from her bag and put over her head when she was caught in a downpour. If she didn't meet up with the once-a-day bus, she would hitch a ride if a car or truck came by.

Mainly, Dorothy set out early in the morning and would stop and talk with any peasants she met on the roads. When she found a trail off the TA, she welcomed the shade of the forest as she looked for settlers. She asked each person she met if they knew where others lived. Little by little, she became known as she drew people together.

Dorothy described her work in the early 1980s in an interview with her friend Sister Barbara:

Our whole emphasis at that time was to help those small groups, isolated out there in the woods, to create strong communal ties, and once they were created, to build strong base Christian communities. . . . There were no villages. . . . It was important . . . for the people to identify themselves publicly as organized. So we worked on creating infrastructure — a school, a little parish center, roads that went into the forest . . . little stores.

A small village of homes

When she had a small group together, Dorothy talked about the power and strength of communities. Together they studied the Gospels for inspiration. Someone, at first Dorothy, would lead a reflection on the situation at hand. She spoke about how they could stand together in the face of crises — disease, lost jobs, and, of course, land struggles.

"Every time we got together," Dorothy wrote, "the subject was land — how much land we could occupy . . . extending more and more into the woods."

One young Brazilian woman, Sandra, explained her gratitude to Dorothy: "I was very young when we met Dorothy. My parents were one of the original families to come to the eastern section of the TA. A large farmer had hired them to cultivate his land, but after a short time he stopped paying them. He would not let them leave and they had no money to run away."

Dorothy asked the community to sell crops and chickens and anything they could afford to raise money for two of their own members, Sandra's parents, so they could be free to buy their own plot of land. Dorothy added a little donation she had received from her family, and INCRA helped them to get title to the plot. They eventually paid back the community and they still farm in Anapu today.

When a community came together, the people usually built a chapel and a school. Sometimes a school was no more than a space in someone's home where one, who could read, taught the others. Dorothy looked forward to a day when a real school with classrooms could be built for the peasants and their children.

One man asked Dorothy why a school was so important when they had to grow crops to feed their families and watch out for intruders. Ever the teacher, she said, "In addition to reading scripture and taking strength from it, you will be able to read road signs and vote for council members who support you in elections."

"Sister, many of us are too old to learn to read and we have no roads and no one to vote for."

"We can change that," she said. "And your children must learn to read."

CHAPTER TWENTY

Centro Nazaré

SEVERAL TIMES during that first year, Dorothy traveled to Nazaré. From the first time she saw Nazaré, she knew it could be much more than a distribution warehouse. She dreamed of building an education center where people from all over the forest could come together to learn the skills they needed to survive. Nazaré was located in just the right place on the river Xingu.

At first, she loved the voyage by boat and bus from Altamira to Nazaré because it gave her time to reflect on the forest's beauty and to think about her plan. She carried her sleeping hammock and stayed overnight with Paulo and his wife or a family in another community. However, she soon told Bishop Krautler that she would like to live closer to Nazaré. She could spend less time traveling, meet more peasants, and create more communities that way. She also thought that she could put her plans in place for a large community center. The bishop agreed as long as she had company; Sisters or lay women came to live and work with her at different times.

A group of farmers built her a small hut of strong, spindly tree trunks lashed together with vines. They made the roof of Babaçu, which are large palm leaves. Her home was a hut like every other settler's hut. Inside was a table, a chair, hooks for her hammock, and a few shelves for books and her other modest belongings.

Once Dorothy had moved in, she began gathering construction materials in any way that she could. She had some money

Centro Nazaré

set aside from her family, and she received grants and donations from friends as well. The workers built dormitories and a new kitchen, and they put a roof over the dining room, which would double as a large meeting hall. Teachers and students could eat and meet together even during the rainy season.

When the education building was finished, many peasant settlers, men and women, applied to come to Centro Nazaré to learn to read and write. They could also learn farming techniques, how to cook more nutritious meals, and how to be leaders in community development. Dorothy was thrilled. By 1989, almost sixty landless peasants — many who had never read nor written before — graduated from the center as teachers.

But success frequently stirred up conflict for Dorothy. The future of Centro Nazaré itself was threatened when a community member, Horatio, tried to take over the center's land. A former landless peasant himself, Horatio farmed the neighboring acres. While he liked Dorothy, he was more impressed and influenced by rich ranchers who lived nearby. Afraid of the influence this Sister had over the peasants, the ranchers frightened Horatio. "She is teaching the peasants that the land is theirs if they just settle on it," they told him. "You should be careful and get a deed to the land."

Horatio came to Dorothy and told her that the center and the crops around it were on his property. "You know Sister," he said, "the law says that landless peasants can only settle where land is not being used productively. I am farming my land." He told her that officials from Belém had come and measured, and Nazaré was, in fact, on his land.

Dorothy guessed that Horatio had arranged for the survey himself and that it was not accurate. She wanted to find out what the real story was. After writing three times to the land office in Belém and getting no response, she took a slow-moving bus to the city. She arrived after the office was closed.

Disappointed but undeterred, she slept overnight on a bench in the outer office, waiting for the doors to open the next morning. When the administrator arrived, he woke her up.

"Sister Dorothy? What are you doing here? I don't believe we had an appointment?"

Dorothy sat up, smoothed her hair, and said, "Good morning, Senhor." She flashed her legendary smile. "I am here because I sent you three letters asking to clarify for us the area where Centro Nazaré's land stops and our neighbor's begins. Since I have heard nothing from you, I thought I might come myself." She got up from the bench and waited for his reply.

"I have never seen the letter, Sister," he said, unlocking the door.

Dorothy waited until he had settled into his desk. She sat in front of him while he attempted to look for her letter in a pile of papers. After a few minutes watching the director fumble with the papers, she said, "Let me help you. I am sure I can find my request." She lifted one paper after another out of the pile, and in a moment she was able to hand him the most recent of her letters. Plainly, it requested clarification of the title to the land at Centro Nazaré.

The man was surprised and shocked. When he recovered, he insisted there was no clear information to give — even with the survey — and that was why he had not written her back. Discouraged and a little tired, Dorothy left for home.

Back at Centro Nazaré, at a community meeting, she presented the idea of moving the building. The uproar was deafening. Community leaders from a few groups were in total disagreement.

"Look at all the time we spent building it," one man yelled. Another said, "We're not moving. You teach us to stand up for our rights; we should stay." In the end, they did not move, and eventually the diocese was able to purchase the land outright.

Uncertainty and disputes were always interrupting community life in the Amazon. In fact, they *are* life in these communities.

CHAPTER TWENTY-ONE

Needed: Strong Men, Strong Women

EARLIER THAT YEAR, with Dorothy's help, local farmers formed an organization called the Pioneers' Association. As a group, they became larger and stronger as more and more members joined. Dorothy had worked with them to draft a request for wider roads and street signs to be located in the forest settlements. Wider roads meant farmers' trucks could carry goods to and from market more easily. Street signs were a symbol of community stability. This was exactly what illegal ranchers did not want.

When these requests received no response from INCRA, the Pioneers Association decided to hold a camp-in, a demonstration in a field outside of town. On a Friday evening, the day of the camp-in, the Brazilian Sisters of Notre Dame de Namur had gathered in Altamira for a meeting and dinner. The Sisters were laughing and telling stories, happy to be together after several months of working in different cities. Dorothy had not planned to go to the site so as not to miss the meeting. She had already done her work with the Pioneers.

Bishop Krautler had met with the farmer-leaders the week before. He agreed that their demands were right and fair and told them he would say a Mass at the site. He would drive his truck and take along a Priest and a young woman who worked for him; both would assist at Mass.

The Sisters' dinner was interrupted by a loud knocking. Dorothy expected it to be someone bringing news about the day, perhaps even the Bishop himself. Instead, she looked outside and saw a man standing there in tears. She pulled him into the house and closed the gate.

"It's the Bishop," he gasped, "he's been in a serious accident."

"Our Bishop D. Erwin . . . was going to this camp-in," she wrote to Maggie. "They had gone some 23 kilometers — about 14 miles — and were going up a steep incline. . . . A truck was coming down. All of a sudden our Bishop saw the truck aim for him. The next thing we knew there was a man here in Altamira, asking for the priest's house. . . . I offered to help."

"The steering wheel saved our Bishop, but his chest, back, mouth, nose area . . . are much offended. We do not know too well as yet how he is as he was flown to Belém . . . to a larger hospital. A priest who was riding in the truck was killed."

Soon after the accident, Dorothy met with some disheartened leaders of the farmers' association. One said, "We know certain ranchers are to blame — they have threatened us before. But why ambush the *Bishop*?"

"To scare you — to remove one of our leaders," said Dorothy.

Another farmer nodded. "What about you, Sister? You have received threats." Dorothy told them she was not afraid and would carry on as long as the Bishop wanted her there.

She asked them if, despite this struggle, they thought that they had a better and healthier life in Nazaré than they would have digging food out of garbage piles or living in isolation and poverty. They were silent for a while. Then one farmer said, "I think we do have better lives, Sister, but it takes strong men and women to throw off the fear of pain and death."

Dorothy had to agree.

CHAPTER TWENTY-TWO

Mobilizing for Change

DOROTHY WAS on the move again. The violence against Bishop Krautler only confirmed her commitment to justice. She wrote to a friend, "Life is now 90 miles per hour."

Timber ranches and sawmills had sprung up near the small town of Anapu. Yet, there was little work for peasants in the town, and scores of them pushed further into the forest. Dorothy followed right along. She moved further east to the outskirts of the town and, with her charismatic style, built more and more communities.

A Sister and two laywomen inspired by her work came to live with her. They divided into teams: Dorothy began the process by gathering settlers into communities; the other Sister taught adults their religion; and the laywomen helped by teaching the boys and girls.

In a short time, Dorothy had hundreds of farmers willing to stand up and fight for their rights. During the summer of 1991, Dorothy, with leaders from INCRA, the CPT, and other organizations, mobilized a large group of peasants to demand more financial aid for Anapu. Prices were rising, and jobs were few. One young farmer cried, "I can't celebrate our annual Field Workers' Day [July 25th]. Even with my rice crop I can't . . . buy a change of clothes. I am destitute."

In October, 360 families boarded busses and traveled the TA for more than 600 miles. Dorothy and other supporters accompanied them. First, they went to Belém, and they then moved

A community gets ready for the settlers' mobilization

on to Brasilia, the country's capital. They carried flour, beans and rice, pots and pans, and wood for fires; they did all their own cooking along the way.

By day, they marched in front of government buildings; they held colorful homemade banners and signs. At night, they ate together and sang songs of unity and hope.

> This struggle is ours
> This struggle is the peoples'.
> It is with justice that we will build a new world.

They slept in tents in parks and washed in the fountains, hanging up shower curtains on poles so that people might clean themselves in privacy.

One day, in Brasilia, the men lay down on the sidewalk and, with their bodies, spelled out "Transamazonica will not wait any more." The radio and television reporters loved it, and eventually the Brazilian president and the various ministers of health, education, roads, and finance responded to the people's demands.

When the farmers of Anapu received funding weeks later,

A family waits to march with Dorothy

Dorothy heaved a sigh of relief. Dorothy and the other organizers were heroes.

She was pleased — and tired. "I have been working on the TA for ten years with few breaks," she told her brother David. She decided it was time for a retreat, and she would go to a University Institute in Oakland, California. There, she would have a chance to study, meditate, and reflect on the challenges to her life in Anapu and the Amazon. She would go in early 1992.

As her plane flew over northern Brazil, the clouds below looked like dirty snow, topped in a brownish grey veil from the smoke of burning brushfires. Now and then, in clearings between the clouds, she could see miles of barren brown land that had once been covered with vegetation.

Words written by Sister Claire, the head of missions for the order, came back to her: "In . . . my air journeys around Brazil . . . I was introduced to the alarming devastation of the tropical rain forests. . . . It is being depleted faster than it can regenerate and, from the little I viewed, destroyed beyond hope of renewal. I felt helpless until I realized that our Sisters are there trying to make a difference."

Dorothy was overcome with the same terrible sadness she had felt on her way to Jacunda. How can people do this to the rain forest? Anger boiled up when she viewed the vast loss of greenery — the "lungs of the world" — and when she thought about the slaughter of animal species and the destruction of plants that held healing potential. It nearly made her physically ill.

"How to help the people recapture a relationship with Mother Earth that is tender and kind?" she wrote to her sister Maggie. She was determined to convince both the government and the small farmers of their responsibility for saving Brazil's Amazon. She sympathized that the peasants' everyday needs made it hard for them to plan for the future. *But they must,* she thought.

In California, at the Institute, Dorothy studied and talked with new friends about the environment. She wept when she told them about the farmers' struggles and the destruction of the surrounding forest. Dorothy believed that, like the Native American tribes and other indigenous peoples in many cultures, the forest and land are sacred and must be cared for. What some ranchers did was sinful. There was no disagreement. Dorothy felt so happy to be among like-minded friends.

She relaxed, prayed with the group, swam in the ocean, and dabbled in art. In February, she visited her sister Maggie. Maggie said that, despite the cold weather, Dorothy took an hour walk each day. "I think that was part of her faith," she said — to be out reflecting and reveling in nature.

Together they watched the Winter Olympics on television. Dorothy said that she thought the people she admired most in the world were Olympic champions. Surprised, Maggie asked why.

Dorothy explained, "Because, from an early age, they are very focused on a goal."

CHAPTER TWENTY-THREE

Dorothy's Goal

BY JUNE 1992, Dorothy was back in Brazil. She was invited to be a delegate to the United Nations Earth Summit in Rio, the first and largest environmental conference ever held. Sister Dorothy Stang was already known in northern Brazil as an environmental champion. Now she would meet other "green" advocates from all over the world.

Approximately 30,000 people attended the twelve-day meeting. Inside the halls, presidents, prime ministers, and leaders of 100 countries exchanged testimony about climate change, biological diversity, and forest protection. Each night, heated discussions took place in hallways, bars, and restaurants. The topic? How to solve the problem of deforestation in Brazil, the Philippines, India, and Southeast Asia. In each country, forest depletion was taking place at a rapid pace.

Some poor people, artists, and activists were not invited into the meetings; they were clustered in the street. Dorothy marched and chanted with them, too, saying, "The death of the forest is the end of our lives." Fervently, she wanted to see Brazilians respect their forests.

Sustainable development was the key: it was possible to use land to answer the human need for food, clothing, and shelter and still preserve the land for future generations. Dorothy thought that this was exactly what the small farmers could and should do within their communities.

She returned to Anapu bursting with passion and full of fresh

Dorothy, the environmental advocate

ideas. The world was finally concerned about the destruction of the rain forests around the globe — or so she thought. She spoke enthusiastically in the villages and communities.

"Many citizens of the world believe as we do in our right to the sustainable development of forest lands," she said. "We must develop our land carefully to meet our needs with crops and farm animals, and plant seedlings to bring back the forest. At the same time, we will be preserving our surroundings so this beautiful universe will be here for our children."

But one farmer was echoed by many in a community meeting, "Sister, you know we struggle to feed our families daily. We have to cut down *some* acres of trees and burn the ground to make space to grow crops. We don't have time to plant trees too.

I think the Earth Summit gave you good ideas but I don't think they are practical."

Dorothy jumped to her feet. "It may not seem practical to you now, Senhor, but when you understand that you may lose the entire forest — and the land — in which you live, you will think again about what I am saying."

She wrote home: "It is not easy to change the work habits of hundreds of years."

CHAPTER TWENTY-FOUR

Anapu Is Growing

DOROTHY HELD onto her high hopes of reforestation despite the farmers' resistance to change. She was convinced that slowing the slash-and-burn techniques of the Amazon farmers and improving reforestation were part of her mission.

Still, her major work was trekking through the forest to find settlers whom she would invite to meetings. The numbers of communities continued to increase, and she knew she would be able to do more if she had a team to continue the work.

Dorothy had her secret wishes. She wrote, "Someone needs to take over my work—I can't do all of this anymore." In the summer of 1995, two young Brazilian women, Maria and Sandra, both about the age of twenty, came to live with Dorothy and lend her a hand in community development. They had met the Sister years earlier.

"She had a very contagious smile," says Maria, "and she loved children. I was eight when I met her the first time and I liked her immediately, so I was happy to go live with her."

Sandra says, "I never gave a thought to becoming a nun, I just liked the work she did, and the way she related to us. She dressed like the people; she ate like the people and slept like the people." Maria and Sandra, working with another Sister, Katy, taught catechism, worked with children and teens, and took up some of the burdens of Dorothy's work.

Because of this help, Dorothy had some time to pursue other projects. But first, she had to pay for them. Her salary from the diocese covered living expenses, and her family was generous

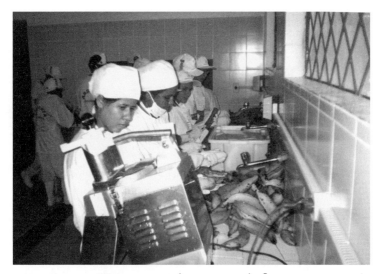

Women prepare bananas to make flour

with gifts. However, she had so many ideas to undertake that she had to look further for funding. One source was the Peace and Justice Committee of a Catholic church in Springfield, Ohio; the members were inspired to adopt her projects, and they supported her with donations for many years.

It was a highly productive time for Dorothy. In one letter to her Ohio Sisters, she explained: "We want to run a small fruit processing industry and we are asking the government to finance . . . a dam for water to flow . . . to support the machinery. We also want to establish a wood craft industry for tables, chairs, doors. . . . Then, part of our work . . . is to help the peasant farmers develop sustainable 'family farming.' Milk is a very desirable product which they can sell."

Dorothy delighted in the women's groups that were forming in spite of Brazil's male-dominated, "macho" culture. One group was planning a fruit-processing factory. Others were studying herbs and plants to be used in place of expensive medicine. Still another group researched infant care and new mothers' health issues.

"Also, I have sent a bright young community member to computer school to get us into the third millennium," she said. "Someone has to know about the new technology," she added, and she bought a computer.

Dorothy was also able to send five Brazilian high school graduates to an agricultural program about 600 miles away. They returned two years later to Anapu to teach settlers the new science and technologies of farming.

In the summer of 1995, Dorothy's sister Maggie and her husband, Elmer, visited Anapu. As Dot showed them around her villages, she bubbled over with enthusiasm about the new projects.

When they arrived at two new school buildings, Dorothy stopped and beamed. She had been able to acquire all the supplies they needed to build two new schools on the TA. The money had come from family, friends, and some grants. "The farmers built the schoolrooms themselves," she told Elmer. "The school officials from Belém call them 'the best-built schools they have ever seen in the Amazon.'" These new schoolhouses were one of Dorothy's proudest achievements, though she gave all of the credit to the builders.

She also told her family about her idea for future reforestation. She had induced a few community leaders to share her vision. She bought hundreds of seedlings in little pots so that farmers could begin to reforest some of their land. "Cut a tree, plant a tree," was her slogan. She asked Maggie to pray that, in time, all small farmers would feel this way and join the struggle for reforesting the Amazon.

Her mood turned a bit, though, when her family was about to go back to the United States. Maggie and Dorothy went for lunch at a small local restaurant in the town of Anapu. A ranch hand and his partner approached their table. Maggie remembers feeling fearful.

Dorothy, proud of the school building going up

"Are you Dorothy Stang?" one asked Dorothy in Portuguese. "I am," she replied. She got up from the table and walked him to the door.

"You should be careful Sister . . . and go home to the United States." He added: "We will get you, you know." The two men glared at the women and walked away.

Maggie asked what he had said. Dorothy brushed it off, saying, "Oh, it happens all the time. What could they possibly want with me?"

Her bravery, however, was a cover-up, and Maggie knew it. Maggie noticed that Dorothy's cheerful mood was subdued a bit as they left the restaurant. Maggie tried to talk with her.

"Why do you stay?" she asked.

"I am needed here," Dorothy told her, and the conversation ended. In private, Maggie and Elmer wondered how many times she had received these threats.

And Maggie was not the only one worried about her sister. In October Dorothy received a letter from the head of the Ohio Diocese's mission office: "We read about the assassination of the Austrian missionary, Father Humbert Mattle in Pará. Naturally our thoughts turned to you. . . . How far are you from the Altamira Church? Are you experiencing tension to the point of violence within your area?"

Dorothy almost smiled at the understatement. She had seen violence increase in proportion to the number of settlers living in her communities. She wrote back: "Violence has never diminished; it is intensifying . . . changing methods. . . . There are no jobs. . . . This generates violence of all kinds."

She did not tell him about the murder of another Priest, killed in an ambush that was meant for her friend Bishop Krautler. She was accustomed to withholding information about the violence she faced. She did not want anyone to suggest she should leave for safer territory. Secretly, she admitted it was frightening. However, she believed it was more dangerous for the peasant people whom she loved so much.

CHAPTER TWENTY-FIVE

Downs and Ups in Pará

DOROTHY HAD convinced peasant farmers to stand up against deforestation and in favor of legal land development. From time to time, these farmers traveled with Dorothy to Belém and Brasilia to testify in Congress about climate change and about the plight of the peasants in the Amazon. Dorothy wanted to show the legislators the strong will and earnest faces of these peasant farmers. She was building support for her dream project.

In the late 1990s, the idea of a federally funded, sustainable development project caught on. Sister Dorothy, the farmer-leaders, INCRA, and other organizations began to work together. Known as the Project for Sustainable Development, or PDS, these are large tracts of land reserved for small farmers rather than for large Brazilian and international agricultural businesses.

This program, supported and protected by the government, would grant small farmers the land they needed to plant crops and raise farm animals for themselves and for sale. The farmers also had to agree to plant a high volume of tree seedlings and reforest much of the land that had been cut by the timber trade. Some senators and lawyers supported the idea of a small farm movement. However, many large ranchers of the area were enraged by the idea of this project. They tried to block it any way they could. Every farm family knew this. One community member asked Dorothy, "Sister, do you really think the neighboring ranchers will not bother us when they see us planting trees and settling in even more than before?"

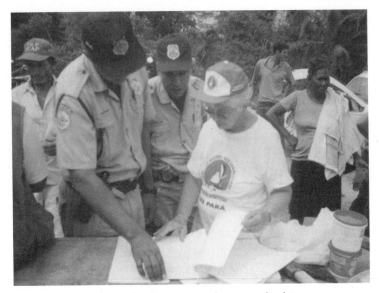

INCRA officials and Dorothy review deeds

Dorothy said, "I know they will try to harass you as they have in the past. What I also know is you are as entitled as the ranchers to the land here and to a productive place in society."

In Anapu, the new year of 1996 brought something to celebrate. Dorothy wrote an excited letter home in January: "Our governor officially signed our area, Anapu, on the Transamazonica, as a county. A great year for Anapu! We can elect a mayor and council people. We have been at it since '88!"

With the help of the CPT lawyers and INCRA, Dorothy had guided farmers through the laborious process of applying to be a county. Some men did not read or write but they signed their names with an X. The Farmer's Association could become a legal union. A few active members wanted to run for office, and now they could. Dorothy had promised them that their hard work would be rewarded, and she was thrilled for them.

There were joyful celebrations, pig roasts, and singing of

Poster urging people to vote.

songs, and then the elections were held. Two farmers won seats on the county council. In addition, the new mayor asked Dorothy, with her team of teachers, to run Anapu County's educational program in the schools.

"This has been long, hard work," Dorothy wrote to Maggie. "Thanks to Exodus and other Biblical studies, people begin to assume their destiny. Where to from here?"

CHAPTER TWENTY-SIX

"I Am Not Afraid"

MORE AND MORE families who wished to make a better life for themselves came to the area around Anapu. More families meant more struggles. Dorothy wrote to the Ohio mission office in January 2002. "Just wanted to give you a sense of our day-to-day life," she told them. "We have at present 500–600 families that migrated this year to Anapu from depleted and droughting areas. Our road was bettered and this is bringing these families."

The new families encountered trouble. They were unfamiliar with life in the forest and unprotected by any government agency.

"We receive in our home groups of men running to us from the woods asking for our support," Dorothy continued. "They and their small families are threatened." Again, ranchers' men were showing them fake documents to get them off the land.

Dorothy did not take these assaults lightly. She knew what had to be done. Tirelessly, she wrote letters and filed a number of formal complaints with the officials in Belém.

In the late 1990s and early 2000s, Dorothy and one or two community leaders traveled to Belém, Pará, the state capital, and even to Brasilia to appear before committees in the Brazilian Congress. Now she was clearly recognized as a champion of a "small-farm movement," and she testified in favor of this economic model — the PDS — for Anapu and the entire Amazon.

She would usher her friends through the security check.

When the guards saw Dorothy, they smiled. They knew that all they would find in her old carrying bag were a few papers and her Bible. In the committee rooms, she spoke in a soft yet determined voice, raising it when she spoke of peasants' human rights and illegal ranchers. She still wore her favorite T-shirt, which read, "Death of the forest is the death of us all."

Patiently, she repeated her mantra, perhaps at times allowing her voice to betray her frustration: "If peasants farm sustainably and support themselves, they can also reforest the rich and magnificent Amazon."

Dorothy's higher profile increased the number of enemies who were determined to stop her. She told her brother David that, on her last visit to Brasilia, "several senators took me aside and warned me to stop speaking out against the ranchers. They were afraid for me. Some predicted I could be killed." More than 700 peasants and their allies had been killed since the land reforms began in the 1970s. Despite knowing this, Dorothy never shied away from her duty. She believed in every person's God-given right to own a piece of land and support oneself and one's family. And someone had to show the way and stand up for the value of human life.

A federal prosecutor, Felicio Pontes, who admired Dorothy and knew her well, cautioned her, "Please be careful, Sister. Do not put yourself in harm's way any more than you have. We need you, Sister. Won't you let the police give you a guard?"

Dorothy refused personal protection. Instead, she wanted protection for her farmers. "I am not afraid for myself. I fear for the lives of these poor people, and if I can help them save their own lives, I will continue my work. The rural peasants have a right to a place in society as much as the wealthy do."

She wrote a letter to Sister Elizabeth Bowyer, then Provincial, in Cincinnati: "I am here today in Altamira. . . . I am . . .

visiting the colonel of the military police [for the area]. . . . We try to relay to the police what is happening as a protective measure. They never go into the woods to get the gunmen but we have to prove that they were informed if anything happens."

She was totally committed to the cause, and she was stubborn and brave.

CHAPTER TWENTY-SEVEN

Dorothy Turns Seventy

IN 2001 Dorothy was seventy years old. In a letter to her Sisters, she wrote, "Whoopee! I'm 70. Thank you, my good God, for LIFE filled with friends and wonderful adventures, sharing, caring, laughing, crying, struggling, and arriving with all of you."

Maria, the young Sister who worked with Dorothy, says, "Even in the midst of great difficulty, she never stopped smiling, playing, dancing . . . eating ice cream."

Still, the hard working conditions had begun to take a toll on her body. Her back often ached. She wore dark glasses all the time because of a degenerative eye condition. And, she had to swap her sandals for stronger walking shoes — she could not walk for as long or as far as she once did.

Around her, the land struggles were growing more difficult. With each influx of settlers, some ranchers, greedy for more and more land, tormented and burned new farmers out of their homes. Despite this, and the threats she received, Dorothy refused to return to the United States. Her friend Joan asked why she did not return. She said, "It is the people. Their lives are so hard; I cannot leave them. And, I have no family; I am free to do this."

Instead, as a sign of her loyalty to her people, Dorothy became a Brazilian citizen in 2004. She kept her U.S. citizenship, but she wanted to "make a commitment to the country that had given her so much." To her friends she admitted that she thought citizenship might protect her from increasing intimidation.

Dorothy and friends: sitting, Sisters Jane Dwyer, Betsy Flynn and Eliska Durovic; standing, Mary Gillespie, Dorothy Stang, Jo Ann Depweg, Katy Webster, and Brazilian Sisters, Raiminha and Amarilis.

A community rebuilds

When Dorothy visited Ohio, Joan and Maggie saw that her mood had grown more serious. She began reading and listening more often to inspirational books and tapes. She said she needed more "God time." She seemed to be shoring herself up for a greater struggle.

A newspaper article had reported that ranchers had placed a price of $25,000 on her head.

Yet in 2004, things appeared to take a turn for the better. Dorothy's goal, her dream project, had become a reality: the PDS was made an official venture of the Brazilian government. The signed agreement set aside several thousand square acres in Anapu for the PDS, the sustainable development project. Farmers living on the PDS would own the land together. Dorothy was thrilled.

Dorothy also believed the new president, Lula Da Silva, who was elected in 2002, would be good for the small farmers and peasants living in the forest. Lula had working-class roots himself, and this gave Dorothy hope that he would support and protect the PDS.

Experienced Amazon farmers were invited to apply to INCRA; each would receive a 250-acre tract of land. They had to promise to reforest 80 percent of their land by planting tree seedlings; they were to use the other 20 percent to grow crops and raise farm animals to sustain themselves and to sell at markets. INCRA would administer the project, and Dorothy would help with a large education effort. She knew the farmers who were getting the first tracts of land, and she expected that they could succeed — as long as there were no serious obstacles put in their paths.

In 2004 Dorothy was named "Woman of the Year" and made an honorary citizen of the state of Pará. The many friends she had made in human-rights organizations wanted to acknowl-

Preparing the soil
to reforest

Farmers and agricultural workers meet with Dorothy

edge her accomplishments, and she was given the Humanitar-
ian of the Year Award from the Brazilian Bar Association. She
felt the awards really belonged to the people of Anapu, and she
invited many of them to the ceremonies.

Disturbing things were happening, however. The *Liberal*,
a major newspaper in Belém, noted that despite — or because

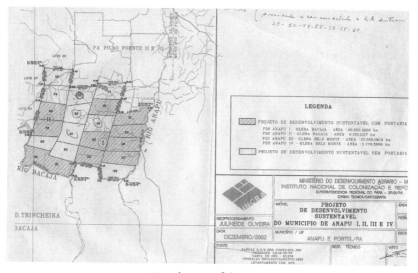

Sample map of the PDS

of—the success in establishing the PDS, Dorothy was "in the crosshairs of ranchers' guns."

In the midst of both celebrations and threats on Dorothy's life, her brother David and sister Maggie arrived in Belém for the awards and stayed in a hotel with her. Dorothy was very happy to have them there. Maggie said the phone never stopped ringing. "A caller would ask for Sister Dorothy, and she would speak with a worried face and be shaking her head. Once the call was over she would say to us, 'You just don't know who to believe.'"

Still, the awards led to an appearance for Dorothy on a television panel where the group was to discuss deforestation in the Amazon and the plight of peasant-farmers. Maggie and David came to the studio with her. She was dressed as usual in a skirt and a T-shirt with the familiar slogan, "Death of the forest is the death of us all." David says, "She was just this little woman with her plain clothes and cloth bag that she carried. Some of the panelists did not pay her too much attention at first."

Dorothy was quiet for a time while the panelists discussed deforestation in the Amazon among themselves. She listened to the panel carefully and thoughtfully. However, something in her had changed. Based on her years of experience and the increasing intimidation she had received, she seemed to believe it was time to take action.

Clearly, the panel did not know what she might have to add. Finally, the female moderator asked Dorothy, "Do you know who these people are that are menacing the farmers?" The woman was shocked by Dorothy's reply.

"I have been in Anapu twenty years," she said. "I know who has land documents that are forged and those that are real . . . and the forgers outweigh the legitimate ones." Then she pulled from her bag a list of ranchers engaged in violence and of police who did nothing for the farmers. She proceeded to read the names. The panelists' eyes popped! Some of the ranchers had ties to large international corporations and to government officials.

Dorothy returned to Anapu and to the PDS. She wanted to get back to work on the new project. Immediately, there was trouble. Ranchers were furious when they heard of her television appearance. Some of them held property close to the PDS. Vitalmiro Bastos de Moura, nicknamed "Bida," was one of these ranchers. He claimed that a farmer, Luis Moraes de Brito, a friend of Dorothy and a leader on the PDS, had been given some of his land.

CHAPTER TWENTY-EIGHT

Trouble on Lot 55

IN DECEMBER, when phone calls were made to Dorothy at the hotel, she had been told about the illegal sowing of grass seed on Luis's land. The workers who sowed the seed insisted it was not Luis's land. This was a common practice — the grass seed grew fast and could take over a farmer's crops in just a week or two. Cattle would be brought in as soon as the grass was ready.

For a time — during January — Luis was able to hold off the intruders. However, things changed in February. Dorothy received a phone call at her house in Anapu. It was Thursday, February 10, 2005. A farmer from the PDS settlement, Esperança, was calling and asking for help. "Luis and his family have been burned out of their home," he told Dorothy. "They need food and clothing and we need your help to decide what to do." The caller said the community would hold a meeting in Esperança to decide what action to take. "Will you come, Sister Dorothy?"

"Of course, I will come," she replied, and she called Ivan, a longtime friend and a community leader, to drive her to Esperança. She would go the next day to bring the supplies and support the settlers as they strategized.

The rancher, Bida, aided by another powerful ranch owner, insisted that he possessed the land where Luis had set up his farm. Luis did not yet have the deed to his acreage on Lot 55 even though he had lived there for four years. INCRA told them that he would receive the papers to this lot in the near future. The map for the property was out of date and unclear.

Most Brazilians celebrate Carnival during the days before Ash Wednesday at the beginning of Lent. In 2005 Ash Wednesday was in early February. The week before, Luis went away with his family to visit relatives. While he was away, two hired gunmen, Rayfran and Clodoaldo, and a third man, Tato — all workers on Bida's ranch — went to Luis's house and waited there for his return.

When Luis returned, Tato, the spokesman, insisted that Bida had sold him the land. Tato offered Luis money to leave the area. Luis refused and instead made the following proposal: "We will go to the office of INCRA together; if your title is legal, I will leave the land. If mine is legal, you will leave."

Tato refused this offer and left. A few days later, Tato returned. He brought in guns and kerosene and two other men. After one night of threats and gunfire, Tato said to Luis, "Go outside — all of you — unless you want to burn in your home."

Luis's family scurried outside, holding a few belongings. Adults and children watched as flames ate up their home and destroyed their abundant crops.

CHAPTER TWENTY-NINE

Dorothy Arrives to Help

ON FEBRUARY 11, 2005, Ivan drove Dorothy from Anapu to Esperança. She was not her usual, positive self. She was quieter and more serious. When Dorothy arrived, she was greeted warmly by community members with hugs and handshakes. Their mentor was here. Food was cooking on the fire. She handed over the clothes and supplies for Luis. He was not there, but members of the community had gathered to see what she thought of the situation. Mostly she listened and said little.

Before this devastation, Luis and some other farmers had built a large lean-to near his home. It was to be the meeting place for the Esperança settlement. Now, Dorothy and a group of friends went down a trail to check out this open-air structure. It had also been destroyed by Tato and his men.

On the site, men were building a house for Tato. Dorothy produced maps to show that this area was part of the land given to the farmers by the government. It was PDS land. Tato got angry. He said to Dorothy, "Sister, you have meddled in our land for long enough. If you don't go away, you will be killed and we will bury you under the building!"

Dorothy had heard threats before, but now her heart pounded in her chest and she said a silent prayer for strength. On the way back to the settlement, the farmers recognized the two *pistoleiros* — gunmen — sitting on a log and pointed them out to Dorothy. She approached them and perched on the same log; she spread the maps out on the ground and pointed to the area, showing them the land that was rightfully Luis's. Then she looked them in the eye and said, "Come to our meeting tomorrow."

She smiled and repeated her invitation. "You know, you could have your own land here."

They looked at the maps and stared at each other. They muttered that the land belonged to their boss. Dorothy stood up, extended her hand and gave them a blessing. With that, they got into their truck and pulled away into the dusky night.

Two nights before, when she was still in Anapu, she had spoken by phone to her brother David in Colorado. "This one will be difficult," she said.

Her usual resting place in Esperança was occupied and she was invited to sleep at the house of another settler, Vicente. Vicente said he wanted to talk with her. During the night, the two gunmen came to Vicente's house. They peered in between the slats of a window, but it was too dark for them to see where she was and they left. Dorothy's back had been bothering her, and she chose not to sleep in a hammock; instead, she had unrolled a mat on the floor underneath the farmer's hammock.

The question remains: How did they know in which home Dorothy was sleeping?

She slept restlessly until daybreak, when she awoke. She had worried about Luis and the other families, and perhaps she wondered about her own fate. She said her morning prayers and dressed. She planned to meet up with her friend Cicero on the road to the meeting.

CHAPTER THIRTY

Morning Dawns:
A Terrible Day

RAIN WAS FALLING lightly as she left for the meeting. The road was muddy. She carried the maps, some letters, and her Bible. A few yards down the road, she passed the home of Cicero and called to him. He was not quite ready to leave. He told her to go ahead and he would catch up.

Twenty minutes is all they needed, she figured. Twenty minutes to walk and talk about the situation. She feared this meeting would not end well, but she was going to try.

And then it happened. Cicero had not yet reached Dorothy. When she got to the top of a hill, Tato's two *pistoleiros*, Rayfran and Clodoaldo, stepped out. Cicero ducked behind a tree. He couldn't see what they carried, but he could hear Dorothy.

"Good morning, gentlemen," she greeted them. Once again she explained that what they were doing was illegal — spreading fast-growing grass seed over a farmer's rightful land. Again she offered her hand and invited them to the meeting. They were silent and she passed by them.

One of the men called out: "Sister Dorothy!" She turned and saw a revolver in his hand. She reached into her bag.

He taunted her. "Are you reaching for your weapon?"

"This is my weapon," she said, pulling out her Bible. She began to read from the Beatitudes in the Gospel of Matthew: "Blessed are the poor in Spirit; the reign of God is theirs. . . . Blessed are the sorrowing; they shall be consoled."

Rayfran looked at his partner, then back at her.

Dorothy continued, "Blessed are the lowly; they shall inherit the land. Blessed are the peacemakers . . ."

Rayfran couldn't bear to hear any more. He readied the gun with a click. Dorothy raised her hand as if to ward off a blow.

The first bullet hit her in the hand. She fell, face forward, holding her Bible.

Rayfran stood over her and, in cold blood, fired five more shots into her back and head. Cicero ran for help.

Because it was the rainy season and the roads were nearly impassable, and because of the lack of telephones in Esperança, eight hours passed before the police arrived. It is said that Dorothy's body never stiffened but was kept soft by the gentle, heavenly rain.

Blessed are you when they insult you and persecute you and utter every kind of slander against you because of me. Be glad and rejoice, for your reward is great in heaven.

Dorothy Stang became a martyr.

Afterword

DOROTHY'S STORY did not end in Esperança. At first, there was the work of getting her body back to Anapu.

A farmer, Reginaldo, jumped on his motorcycle to get the police in Anapu to move the body. Even in death, Dorothy had to wait for officials to act. The officers had all kinds of reasons not to go, claiming that they had no truck and "the roads are too muddy."

The farmer suggested he could get a truck, but the police said, "We are not allowed to drive a civilian's truck."

A call to Felicio Pontes, the federal prosecutor and a friend of Dorothy, put an end to the phony reply. "Go, or else," he said to the police. The truck carrying the officers arrived in Esperança late that afternoon to take her body to Belém.

Several days of mourning followed. Sisters of Notre Dame de Namur from all over Brazil came to Belém, where an autopsy had to be performed. The Sisters told stories of Dorothy, of her sun-flowered dress — her only dress — her smile, and her determination, and they wished they could just hear her laughter one more time. They cried and tried to comfort each other. They helped with the Masses and the funeral arrangements. And they offered what consolation they could to the hundreds of mourners who came to Belém to honor Dorothy and voice their demands for justice.

After Belém, Dorothy's body was taken to Altamira; Bishop Krautler said another Mass for a full church. He was interrupted by a boy coming up the steps to the altar with a message for him. Grimly, the Bishop said, "I have just received news that a Farmer's Union leader in the south of Pará has been killed. Let

Funeral procession of several thousand
mourners led by Bishop Krautler

us pray for him." Some cried out in astonishment, others wept audibly. A ripple of weary understanding passed through the crowd. Someone cried out, "Will the struggle never end?"

The final of four funeral Masses and the burial was at Anapu. Father Amaro, Dorothy's young friend, received her coffin for a Mass of Christian burial. An emotional Padre Amaro admitted that Dorothy "was like a mother to me . . . more than a mother." She had encouraged Amaro to become a Priest and also to return home to help continue her work.

Over 2,000 people walked with Dorothy's casket across a small, swinging bridge to a large, open plaza on the other side of the river. The location seemed appropriate for the loving and lively nun: empty by day, it was an open-air club at night — a place for dancing and having a good time.

Dignitaries from Belém and settlers from the Amazon had come to the Anapu River to see Dorothy laid to rest in the forest. Some people had walked for twenty miles to be there. Others came on bicycles and motorcycles. There were men on crutches and women carrying tiny babies. They were all Dorothy's people. They loved her deeply and missed her profoundly.

One farmer cried out, "She is not buried in Anapu, she is planted!"

Along the route, soldiers stood by with guns ready, offering protection for the people in the event that chaos broke out. It was a protest march; it was a celebration of her life; it was a sorrowful funeral procession for someone who was dearly loved and who had offered her life to bring justice to a violent land.

Justice in Brazil, for other than the rich and powerful, is hard to come by. Of the 700 rural peasant farmers and leaders killed in the Amazon between 1975 and 2005, only three trials for murder were held, and none of the convicted served their sentences in jail.

David Stang and Sisters Rebeca Spires and Ellen De Breio
with reporters before the trial

By the end of 2005, based on testimony by Dorothy's friend
Cicero, the two gunmen had been arrested for Dorothy's murder. They were tried and jailed. In 2006 Tato received the same
judgment. However, the two ranchers suspected of hiring the
gunmen were free to conduct their business. Their guilt was
harder to prove.

But on a May morning in Belém in 2007, with the damp heat
hanging in the air, a historic trial began — that of Vitalmiro
Bastos de Moura, called Bida. It lasted only two days — the custom in Brazil. The courtroom was shocked when Bida's lawyer
pulled the Brazilian flag close to him and shouted, "Dorothy
had the DNA of the American imperialists." He implied that
Dorothy was an American who wanted to take over the Amazon for the United States.

The jury then listened carefully while the prosecutor, Edson
Cardoso, jumped up and shouted, "She was a Brazilian citizen,

Anapu settlers call for justice for all

she was a nun!" He presented the facts eloquently and with great emotion. The jury was further impressed by the testimony of Sister Rebeca. "Dorothy was a woman of integrity ... she never worked on her own," she said. "She was working with the Brazilian government agencies and with the Catholic Church."

When it was over, Bida was convicted on the charge of a conspiracy to murder Sister Dorothy Stang.

Busloads of Anapu peasants and farmers came to the square outside the courthouse. They camped overnight in tents made of black plastic. They waited to hear the courtroom news. From time to time, a sound truck played music or Padre Amaro led a communal prayer for justice.

When the conviction of Bida was announced over the loudspeakers, a roar went up and the celebration began. Songs, dancing, and hugging all confirmed the feeling that justice had been done for Dorothy, for Anapu, and for the poor farmers of Brazil.

Crowds from Anapu wait outside the courthouse

They had rejoiced in 2005, when Rayfran and Clodoaldo were convicted and again in 2006, when the gunmen were joined in jail by Tato, who was convicted of hiring the gunmen.

But now, a rancher — Bida, one of the elite — was to be imprisoned for twenty-nine years. This was a first for the corrupt legal system of Pará. Impunity — that is, freedom from punishment for a privileged class — was finally being tested in Brazilian courts.

The joy was short-lived. In May 2008, exactly one year later, Bida's conviction was appealed and overturned. He is now a free man. And another rancher, Regivaldo Pereira Galvão, is also accused of plotting Dorothy's death. He is still free. Whether or not he will ever be tried remains to be seen.

However, a precedent has been set. Bida, a wealthy rancher from northern Brazil, was tried and convicted of a shocking crime. He has been released from jail, but his case will be appealed on behalf of Dorothy's Sisters, her family, and the State of Pará. Bida's discharge from prison was a setback; however, the legal battle in Pará continues.

More importantly, support continues for the daily struggle of the people who live on the land and cultivate it while respecting the forest. The hope, of course, is that the death of Dorothy and the trials for justice in her case will inspire other victims' families to stand up to corruption in the face of such extreme injustice. There is a popular saying in Brazil: "God's justice may take a while, but it never fails . . . where human justice often fails."

Did Dorothy make a difference? Sister Jane Dwyer, who worked with Dorothy and continues to work in Anapu with Sister Katy Webster, says, "She definitely made a difference in the lives of these peasants. And they will all tell you that. Had Dorothy not come to this part of the Amazon, had she not built schools and taught the people how to read and to come together, I don't think the people would be as strong and committed as they are today, and Anapu would not be the viable community that it is."

Did she die in vain? Definitely not. The news of Dorothy's murder on February 12, 2005, circled the globe. Sister Elizabeth and Sister Joan in the Ohio Province office were barraged by phone calls from Europe, the Americas, Africa, and Asia. Many people would never know or have known of Dorothy's work with Amazon peasants had she not been killed by ranchers acting illegally.

The publicity surrounding the trials shed light on a major unresolved conflict that Brazil still faces: how can peasant farmers and other landless citizens gain the right to ownership of their plots of earth and uphold a responsibility to care for the Amazon? Can they live in harmony with large, neighboring agribusiness farmers and ranchers who seek to control all of the land?

The struggle between poor and disenfranchised peasants and rich, powerful, and illegal ranchers will continue. However,

A woman prays at the grave of Sister Dorothy

many organizations worldwide have recognized Dorothy Stang for her human rights efforts giving greater testimony to the difference she made. Notable is the prestigious United Nations Human Rights Prize, which was presented posthumously to the Sisters and Dorothy's brother, David Stang, in December 2008. This award is given only every five years to a small, select group of activists for justice, peace, and freedom. It is significant that this international body has recognized Dorothy's fight, and it calls attention to the worldwide struggle to preserve the environment and provide a just homeland for all peoples.

When someone so loved and respected dies a violent death, we try to make sense of it. In Dorothy's case — undoubtedly a terrible tragedy — it seems that her life on earth is only a part of the story. Dorothy, like a fire extinguished too fast, has left behind hot coals that keep sending up sparks of inspiration. Books, curriculum guides, films, a play, even an opera have been written

Dorothy's spirit survives

about her. And several young women, including Maria and Sandra, have become Brazilian Sisters of Notre Dame de Namur.

SISTER DOROTHY'S passion for justice never diminished; it is a beacon in a heartless world. In 2000, Dorothy expressed her vision in a letter to her sister Maggie: "If we keep working, helping our people to grow through education, they will have the ability to speak up, organize, and create within themselves a spirit — guided by The Spirit — and a new people."

Did she know she would become a martyr? She wrote to her family, "I might not see this day, but with the help of all of you, our people will grow in their understanding and caring for others. I have to be with these people. If it means my life, I want to give my life."

At the Anapu funeral, one farmer shouted, "Dorothea vive!" — Dorothy lives!

Dorothy Stang gave up her life for others. But her spirit lives in the struggle she kindled for equality, respect, and sustainability.

The author with her "Brazilian daughters," May 2007

Discussion Questions

The following questions can be used with a class, a discussion group or for personal reflection.

1. Sister Dorothy is often referred to as a martyr rather than a victim of murder. How would you describe the difference between the two? In what way did Dorothy give her life, not only at the moment of her death, but each day of her life?

2. Dorothy's sister said that Dorothy was "just plain stubborn." Do you agree? Is being stubborn a weakness of character or a strength? Can you think of any other person who did great things by focusing on a goal? What was Dorothy's goal?

3. What qualities in Dorothy's personality are appealing to you? Can you identify with her in any way?

4. How did Dorothy's early life prepare her for her work in Brazil?

5. Dorothy seemed to be in touch with the God-given dignity of each person. How did this awareness affect the way that she related to people, in particular the people with whom she worked?

6. Dorothy asked her bishop to send her to "the poorest of the poor." He did that by sending her to the landless peasants of Pará. What do you think Dorothy learned about life from the peasant farmers and their families? What impact did she have on their lives?

7. Dorothy had a passionate love for all of nature. She referred to the forest as "those noble trees." When talking about the burning of the forest, she asked, "Have you ever heard the sound of a monkey crying?" Is this personal relationship with nature widespread in our society today? If it were, what difference would it make in regard to the environment?

8. In addition to her personal love for nature, Dorothy had other reasons for wanting to preserve the Amazon rain forest. What would be your reasons for preserving the forest? In what ways was Dorothy's vision global?

9. How does the destruction of the Amazon and other rain forests impact our lives in the northern hemisphere? What can we do to help put a stop to this destruction?

10. Dorothy Stang spent much of her life advocating for social justice. What is social justice and what are the ways she advocated for it?

11. Dorothy experienced the dramatic differences between the rich and the poor in Brazil. What are these differences and how did she try to improve the conditions of the poor?

12. Much of Dorothy's life was focused on the development of communities. What is involved in the building of communities and what are the challenges in trying to build community?

13. When she first went to Brazil, Dorothy could be said to be a "stranger in a strange land." How did Dorothy stop being a stranger and became more and more a Brazilian? Have you ever experienced feeling like an "outsider" and what did you do about it?

14. While the United States is considered an industrialized nation, Brazil is still going through the process of industrialization. Explain the ways Brazil is making progress towards industrialization and the ways it is still an agricultural society.

15. Clothing is an important symbol of one's position. What is the importance of uniforms and how does changing one's uniform lead to changes in the ways people see you? What happened when the nuns changed their traditional habits to adjust to the Brazilian weather?

16. Dorothy said, "My faith sustains me." What do you think she meant?

17. What did Dorothy actually accomplish in her lifetime? Her pastor said that she is accomplishing even more now, after her death. What do you think he meant?

18. Will having read this book change your life? How?

Chapter Notes

These chapter notes provide additional background information.

FOREWORD

The Sisters of Notre Dame de Namur (SND de N) are an international order of nuns founded in 1804 by Sister, and later Saint, Julie Billart in France with the help of her friend Françoise Blin de Bourdon. Julie, as a result of her deep faith, expressed the belief that poor young women, especially the poor and abandoned, deserved an education, and the two women worked toward that end. Today, the SND de N order works to enable those who are materially poor to obtain what is rightfully theirs by changing unjust structures. The order believes that education in varied forms is the best way to accomplish this goal.

The phrase "to be an option for the poor" has always been the guiding principal for the Sisters of Notre Dame de Namur. Stated in the very first constitution of this order — written by the founder, Saint Julie Billart — "the option for the poor" has meant that the Sisters and their church are always ready to work for the poor by standing up for, teaching, and supporting those living in poverty. The phrase is also central to Vatican II encyclicals and for many people of all faiths who work for social justice throughout the world.

CHAPTER 2. THE EARLY YEARS

This chapter is based largely on interviews with Dorothy's brother David and sisters Barbara and Marguerite.

Henry Stang was engaged in organic farming, in which he emphasized using compost made from vegetable scraps and no chemicals. In the 1930s, however, this type of farming was not common. It is probable that he learned this from his German ancestors, who are said to be among the best farmers in the world.

CHAPTER 3. THE LONG ROAD TO BRAZIL

Missionaries from many religions continue their work today in Latin America, Africa, Asia, and even the United States where help is needed. There are also organizations that offer secular missionary work opportunities, such as the Peace Corps, AmeriCorps, and Greenpeace.

In 1948 and 1949 many missionaries were expelled from the newly formed People's Republic of China, led by Mao Zedong. The new political regime had come to power, and they were not interested in having Americans, much less religious Americans, teaching and influencing Chinese citizens.

CHAPTER 4. ARIZONA, MISSION TERRITORY

In 1912 Arizona became the 48th state to be admitted to the United States. In 1953 there was still a lot of land to be developed, especially around the City of Phoenix. When Dorothy and her Sisters went there in 1953, the population was not quite 1 million. Today, the population is over 5 million. (U.S. Census Bureau information)

According to a website about Mexican farm workers, (http://www.pbs .org/kpbs/theborder/history/timeline/17.html), Mexican workers began coming to the United States in the middle of the nineteenth century, some even before the Civil War. Mexican workers began coming to the area in and around Phoenix, Arizona, about 1920, living in substandard housing and ghetto neighborhoods. By 1953 the conditions were somewhat better, but the migrant families were always poor and in need of education and social services.

Sister Paula Marie, SND de N, who taught in Arizona with Dorothy, and a letter from Joseph Simek, a student of Dorothy's, were helpful in writing this chapter.

CHAPTER 5. A LESSON IN THE FIELD

In general, the pesticide DDT was used widely on crops in the United States between 1945 and 1959. However, beginning in 1959 various restrictions were put on its use, and in 1972 there was a decree that ended the use of DDT as a pesticide for home gardens and crops. This information can be found in DDT: *A Review of Scientific and Economic Aspects of the Decision to Ban Its Use as a Pesticide,* prepared for the Committee on Appropriations of the U.S. House of Representatives by the EPA, July 1975, EPA-540/1-75-022, and in a press release from the EPA (December 31, 1972).

Unfortunately, sprayers of toxic pesticides are still in use in parts of the United States today, and children continue to be born with deformities as a result. See the *Raleigh News & Observer,* September 11, 2008, p. 1 (www.newsobserver.com).

CHAPTER 6. TRAINING IN PETROPOLIS

"Comunidadea eclesiais de base," or base Christian communities, were and remain small groups of Catholic laypeople who study the Bible and apply their reflections on Bible stories to their everyday experiences (Adriance, *Promised Land*). Most of the clergy in Brazil welcomed the opportunity to begin community building in order to educate the poor about their religion and present to them the notion of human rights. Work and pronouncements from Pope John XXIII's Vatican II led to the development of the community movement.

Much of this chapter is derived from journal entries written by Sister Barbara English, SND de N, a colleague and friend of Dorothy and one of the four Sisters who accompanied her to Brazil.

CHAPTER 8. A YOUNG TEACHER EDUCATES THE SISTERS

A Catholic Bishop is the head of a group of churches called a diocese. Coroatá was in the diocese of the State of Maranhão. In the Episcopal Church, women can also be Priests and Bishops.

CHAPTER 10. OUT FROM COROATÁ

The number of peasants who needed to be visited was far greater than the number of clergy in Coroatá. They were not able to visit everyone in one year. Still, they were obliged to try until the base-community movement was implemented. Then groups could meet and say prayers, sing hymns, and practice their religion in between clergy visits.

CHAPTER 11. WORD GETS AROUND

The First Vatican Council had been held in the 1870s, convened to address certain issues the Catholic Church faced in that day. In 1962 the second council called all the Bishops of the Church to Rome to consider the pastoral needs of the worldwide Church and seek ways to implement spiritual renewal.

CHAPTER 12. MOVING TO THE "WILD WEST" OF BRAZIL

Much of this chapter draws on the research of Sister Roseanne Murphy in *Martyr of the Amazon*, specifically chapter 5; and that of Joseph A. Page, *The Brazilians*, p. 296.

Land reform is a recurring issue throughout the world and in Brazil's Amazon region in particular. In the late 1960s and 1970s, the Amazon was opened to all Brazilians. However, "when migrants began to arrive and looked for plots to farm — the dream of every landless peasant — they often discovered . . . that they were settling on property claimed by someone with an . . . apparently valid legal title to the premises" (Page, *The Brazilians*, p. 296).

In an interview with Rebeca Spires, SND de N, she acknowledges that the treatment of indigenous peoples, Brazilian Indians, is as tragic as that of the North American Indians. Like the Brazilian peasant settlers, many indigenous tribes have been pushed around, burned off their land, and wiped out. She continues her work helping to stabilize certain Amazon tribes.

CHAPTER 13. THE NEW CHALLENGES

Dorothy joined the Pastoral Land Commission (CPT) and relied on these lawyers as friends and counselors. The organization is as active today as it was when Dorothy was alive and is very instrumental in preparing the witnesses for the trials of the ranchers and hit men who killed Dorothy and other victims. While it was begun as and remains a Roman Catholic organization, it has always been ecumenical; it works especially closely with the Lutheran Church and those of other faiths who join in the struggle.

CHAPTER 16. THE COURAGE TO CARRY ON

The Institute for Colonization and Agrarian Reform (INCRA) was helpful to Dorothy at times, and at times it became an impediment — often because the group was severely underfunded. They exist today, and information about their work can be found on the Greenpeace website, http://www.greenpeace.org.uk/blog/forests/.

This phrase, and the action of "shifting the pastoral orientation of his area . . . toward the preferential option for the poor," was supported by Bishop Krautler and other Brazilian Bishops responding to Vatican II's edicts (Adriance, *Promised Land*, footnote no. 1).

CHAPTER 18. INCRA'S "BEST STAFF MEMBER"

Peasants were, by law, instructed that they could settle a plot of land that was not being used "productively" — that is, for crops or cattle. This vague but legal statement was the basis of many of the land struggles that took place during this time and continues today.

A story ran in the *New York Times* in September 2005 describing this process of falsifying deeds to plots of land (Rohter, "Brazil's Lofty Promises After Nun's Killing Prove Hollow").

CHAPTER 19. IT'S ALL ABOUT LAND

Sandra and Maria have since become Sisters of Notre Dame de Namur. Sandra is studying to be a lawyer, while Maria is receiving an advanced degree in education. Other young Brazilian women are in formation to become SNDs.

CHAPTER 22. MOBILIZING FOR CHANGE

This song is a familiar one that is often sung at demonstrations in Brazil.

CHAPTER 26. "I AM NOT AFRAID"

The phrase "lungs of the world" is graphic and used by some educators and writers to explain the air quality around the world. The Amazon rain forest and other forests are said to clean most of the carbon dioxide in our air and return fresh oxygen to us. However, some scientists object to the phrase because it simplifies the process.

See the discussion in the *National Geographic Magazine,* January 2007, about Dorothy and the small-farm movement in conflict with large agribusiness farming.

CHAPTER 29. DOROTHY ARRIVES TO HELP

From *Human Rights in Brazil* (2005), p. 24. The author of the article, Antonio Canuto, is secretary of the lawyers' organization (the CPT). Not only were none of the three convicted killers left in jail, but one, a rich man with a chronic illness, was also allowed to rest at his home for the duration of his sentence.

Selected Bibliography

Sister Dorothy's letters to other Sisters of Notre Dame de Namur and her family comprise the main body of research about her life. These documents are archived at Mount Notre Dame in Cincinnati, Ohio. The website for the Sisters of Notre Dame de Namur in Ohio is www.SNDdeNOhio.org

Other materials, used for historical and cultural background information, are listed here.

BOOKS

Adriance, Madeleine Cousineau. *Promised Land: Base Christian Communities and the Struggle for the Amazon.* Albany: State University of New York Press, 1995.

Le Breton, Binka. *A Land to Die For.* Atlanta: Clarity Press, 1997.

Murphy, Roseanne. *Martyr of the Amazon: The Life of Sister Dorothy Stang.* New York: Orbis Books, 2007.

Page, Joseph A. *The Brazilians.* Cambridge, Mass.: DaCapo Press, 1995.

Poelzl, Volker. *Culture Shock Brazil.* Portland, Ore.: Graphic Arts Center Publishing Company, 2003.

Robinson, Alex. *Footprint Brazil.* Fourth ed. Bath, UK: Footprint Books, 2007.

Sydow, Evanize, and Maria Luisa Mendonça, eds. *Human Rights in Brazil 2005: A Report.* São Paulo: The Social Network for Justice and Human Rights, 2005.

Taliani, Alberto. *Brazil.* São Paulo: Manole, 2000.

World Almanac and Book of Facts, 2009. New York: World Almanac Books, 2009.

REPORTS

Carter, Miguel (Director). "Struggling for Sustainable Development in the Brazilian Amazon." Research project for the class "Micropolitics of Development." Washington, D.C., American University of International Service. (Unpublished, 2006).

United Nations General Assembly. Report of the UN Conference on Environment and Development. Rio de Janeiro, 3–14 June 1992. www.un.org/documents/ga/conf151/aconf15126-1annex1.html.

ARTICLES

Barrionuevo, Alexei. "Acquittal in Nun's Killing Provokes Outcry in Brazil." *New York Times*, May 8, 2008. http://www.nytimes.com/2008/05/08/world/americas/08rancher.html.

———. "With Guns and Fines, Brazil Takes on Loggers." *New York Times*, April 19, 2008. http://www.nytimes.com/2008/04/19/world/americas/19brazil.html.

Deegan, Sean. "The Angel of the Amazon: Passionate, Fearless, Eliminated." *Africa* 70, no. 8 (November 2005). St Patrick's Missions, Dublin.

Goldman, Emily. "Brazilian Human Rights Lawyer Addresses Commission." Washington, D.C.: *RFK Memorial* (December 2005). www.brazilnetwork.org.

Groppo, Paolo. "Agrarian Reform and Land Settlement Policy in Brazil: Historical Background." Sustainable Development Department, Food and Agriculture Organization of the United Nations. www.ICARRD-Secretariat@fao.org.

"A History of Brazil." Microsoft Encarta, 2008. www.encarta.msn.com/encyclopedia/Brazil.html.

Hohm, Marguerite, and Susan Hohm. "Dorothy Stang: An Uncommon Life of Justice." *Connection* (November/December 2005).

Hovey, Pauline O. "A Modern Day Martyr." *St. Anthony Messenger* (February 2006).

Jeffrey, Paul. "The Brazilian Amazon: Legacy of an EcoMartyr." *National Catholic Reporter Online*, July 11, 2008. http://ncronline3.org/drupal/?q=node/145.

Johnson, Elizabeth A., CSJ. "God's Beloved Creation." *America*, April 16, 2001.

Lambert, Tim. "A Short History of Brazil." www.localhistories.org/Brazil.html (2006).

McCarty, Mary. Columns about Dorothy Stang and Brazil, *Dayton Daily News*, August 2007.

Patai, Daphne. "A Nun's Tale: An Oral History." *Massachusetts Review* (Fall/Winter 1986). University of Massachusetts, Amherst.

Robertson, Jennifer. "Angel of the Amazon." *OrganicStyle* (October 2005). San Rafael, Calif.

Rohter, Larry. "Brazil Gambles on Monitoring of Amazon Loggers." *New York Times*, January 14, 2007.

———. "Brazil's Lofty Promises after Nun's Killing Prove Hollow." *New York Times*, September 23, 2005.

Wallace, Scott and Alex Webb. "Last of the Amazon." *National Geographic* (January 2007). Washington, D. C.

Index